D1114571

DEMCO

Also by Cheryl Tuttle and Penny Paquette:

Parenting a Child with a Learning Disability
Parenting a Child with a Behavior Problem

Also by Cheryl Tuttle:

Challenging Voices: Writings by, for, and about
People with Learning Disabilities

THINKING GAMES

TO PLAY WITH YOUR CHILD

Easy Ways to Develop
Creative and Critical Thinking Skills

Newly Revised Second Edition

CHERYL GERSON TUTTLE
PENNY HUTCHINS PAQUETTE

LOWELL HOUSE

LOS ANGELES

CONTEMPORARY BOOKS

CHICAGO

Library of Congress Cataloging-in-Publication Data
Tuttle, Cheryl Gerson.
    Thinking games to play with your child : easy ways to develop creative and critical thinking skills / Cheryl Gerson Tuttle and Penny Hutchins Paquette.
        p.   cm.
    ISBN 0-929923-49-9 (1st ed)
    ISBN 1-56565-810-8 (2d ed)
    1. Educational games.   2. Early childhood education—Parent partici-
pation   I. Paquette, Penny Hutchins.   II. Title.
LB1029.G3T88 1991
371.3'078—dc20
                                                            91-17913
                                                               CIP

Lowell House
2020 Avenue of the Stars, Suite 300
Los Angeles, CA 90067

Publisher: Jack Artenstein
Associate Publisher, Lowell House Adult: Bud Sperry
Design: Laurie Young

Manufactured in the United States of America
10 9 8 7 6 5 4 3 2 1

For Jerry and Bob

ACKNOWLEDGMENTS

We would like to thank Judy Jacobi, Charles Gessner, Beverly Clark, Terry Pollack, and Janina Murphy for their contributions to the new edition of this book. We would also like to acknowledge the wonderful teachers in our school system who showed us every day that thinking skills can be taught.

Most of all we would like to express our gratitude to our children—Matthew, Ross, Eric, Danielle, and Michael—who grew up to be such thoughtful adults and helped us prove the techniques in this book can work.

CONTENTS

TWO

WRITE NOW
Helping Your Child Develop Writing Skills 53

THREE

COUNT ME IN
Helping Your Child Develop Math Skills 91

FOUR

WHAT?

FIVE

INVOLVING OLDER CHILDREN   147

TO THE
THOUGHTFUL
PARENT

In the six years since we first published *Thinking Games to Play with Your Child*, more and more information has become available about learning and child development. We believed that playing games with children, interacting with them in positive ways, and becoming involved in their intellectual development at home would make a positive difference for our children.

The recent flurry of child development reports confirmed our original beliefs. Parents can and should be involved in the development of their children. Reading to children, talking to them, and spending time with them will help their intellectual and emotional development. Even though more statistical information supports the importance of active parenting, we still know the job is the most challenging we will ever face.

Being a parent is one of the most difficult professions, and it's the one for which most of us have the least training. Between us, Penny and I have raised five children. Parenthood required us each to be teacher, psychologist, nurse, and coach. We did the best we could, but often we needed help. We called the doctor when we needed medical advice, and we talked to family and friends and looked to self-help books for assistance in the psychological areas. We expected teachers to teach our children all they needed to know to succeed in school, and we expected our children to learn.

When I sent my children off to school at age five, I believed, as my parents did, that school could do everything necessary to give them the skills and confidence they would need to thrive and prosper in higher education and in the adult world. Both as a parent and as a teacher, I soon discovered I was wrong. The schools couldn't do it alone.

It became clear to me that my children were going to need extra support. My older son needed to work on his reading speed; my younger one needed help with his math facts. Both had terrible handwriting. It didn't take me long to realize the classroom teacher did not have the time to give them all the special attention they would need. And that was more than twenty years ago.

Today, the situation is even more difficult. When we were growing up, the entire school day could be devoted to teaching the basics. But now, new problems reduce the number of hours teachers can spend on the development of foundation-level skills. Budget woes are increasing class size, and the teaching day is fragmented by a multitude of offerings that are essential in today's society. In many local public school systems, a portion of every day is spent on important topics such as sex education, drug education, self-esteem development, computer literacy, and crisis intervention. Of course, all these offerings are invaluable, but they also take important time away from developing the basics of reading, writing, math, and the application skills which I call *thinking skills*.

During a typical day at my school system, children are in

school for six hours. Fortunately, it continues to offer important enrichment activities, including gym, art, and music. Like many school systems, we also offer special events and self-esteem development programs. Children spend nearly an hour eating lunch and playing at recess. With these activities, almost half the day is already spoken for. And, during the three hours left, teachers are expected to teach reading, writing, math facts, problem-solving skills, basic geography, and at least some science. Times have changed. Classroom teachers can't do it all. They need help.

As a teacher, I recognize the difference involved parents can make in their child's education. When you read to your child, you automatically improve his vocabulary. When you review homework, you show by your attention that learning is important. But if your family is anything like mine was, finding time to squeeze in one more activity is the ultimate challenge.

If the academic day is fragmented, most family days are even more splintered. Both parents often work outside the home, and many families are managed by single parents. You work, you shop, you do laundry, you fix meals, you may even manage to give a portion of your day to a volunteer project. And even though your children watch a lot of television and at times seem tethered to their computer games, they aren't exactly idle. They are playing soccer and baseball and softball and football. They go to dance class and piano lessons. They have paper routes and dentist appointments, Cub Scout and Brownie meetings. You may recognize the need for at-home academic support but perhaps can't find the time or energy to accomplish one more thing during the day.

When I talk to parents during parent-teacher conferences, they are always eager to do what they can to help their children learn, but they are also frustrated. In addition to having limited time, they often find that their children are not terribly cooperative.

The frustrations are predictable. Children do not view their parents as their teachers. When I tried to help my children with their homework, they were quick to tell me I didn't do it the way their teachers did, and that my way must be wrong.

And, as parents, we have to acknowledge that children would rather work on improving their laser-blasting skills than their classroom skills. Children do not want their parents to take what they perceive as precious time away from their favorite television program or computer game. After an afternoon of homework, they don't want to do more "work" on reading, and they aren't too excited about practicing those math facts.

When my oldest was encouraged to practice his reading at home, he hid his books behind the radiator. Homework became a struggle, and our working together created a tension that was not helpful for either of us. My ego was tied to his learning and his academic achievement, and I got angry when I felt he wasn't trying hard enough. We usually ended our homework sessions shouting at each other. This wasn't the way I had visualized the "enrichment time."

Of course, some schools have managed to offer enrichment programs within the school day—what many schools call *gifted or talented programs*. But what if your child, the one you know has many gifts and a multitude of talents, doesn't quite fit into your school system's definition of *gifted*? What if those programs offer other children the opportunity to go beyond the traditional curriculum and learn to integrate what they have learned, the opportunity to develop those essential thinking skills? Where does that leave your child? It leaves her out.

And where does that leave you, a parent? It leaves you angry and frustrated. And to make matters worse, you feel guilty because you don't think you have the time or the expertise to help.

The good news is that you are wrong. The primary goals of

Thinking Games to Play with Your Child are to help you maximize your child's enthusiasm for learning, to create a desire for him to continue learning, and to help him feel good about himself. And that is not as difficult as you may think.

I originally designed the activities in this book to help my own boys learn the basics and to improve their images of themselves as learners. My first attempts were not as successful as I had hoped. When I began to use these activities, they looked too much like schoolwork and were quickly rejected. It was not until I "packaged" them so they looked more like commercial games that I was able to capture their interest. Children like to play games. I recognized that and used it to my advantage.

Then my children enjoyed that special time with me. We had fun. They looked forward to playing, and they became excited about learning. I was thrilled with our success. Penny and I have written this book to help you have the same positive learning experiences with your child.

I know you can make a difference. Researchers tell us parents are an important resource. In their book, *What Works, Research About Teaching and Learning*, the United States Department of Education states, "Parents are their children's first and most influential teachers." They further explain that parents have the opportunity to do things at home that will help their children succeed at school, but parents are doing less than they might. Their research has shown that mothers spend on average, less than half an hour each day talking, explaining, and/or reading to their children. Fathers, on average, spend less than fifteen minutes.

I'm sure you want to spend more time than average, but you may need guidance and direction. The activities and strategies in this book will provide you with tools to help your child strengthen the skills she is learning at school. The games will improve thinking skills; they will provide structured activities that are both educational and fun; and they will also help both you and your child feel good about yourselves.

The self-esteem of young children is fragile and it needs to be nurtured. The games themselves won't miraculously improve self-esteem, but they will provide you with a way to give positive messages to your child.

If your child knows there will be a time set aside when you will be together, you are showing him he is important and that you want to be with him. Because these games are organized so that there is more than one way to win—by points, by creativity and/or by chance—there are many opportunities for praise and positive reinforcement. We all like to hear good things about ourselves, and when it is said often enough by someone we trust, we begin to believe what we hear.

Most of the games in this book are intended for children in preschool through third grade. The first three sections offer games that enhance reading skills, writing skills, and arithmetic skills, "the three Rs." In this revised edition, we offer a fourth section that focuses on an equally important R—remembering. The final section offers ways to involve your older child with games you and her younger sibling are playing, and also presents some games specifically designed for the older child. Each game includes a discussion of the skills developed while playing, directions for playing the game, the materials needed, the amount of time to allow for play, and suggestions for variations. Under the "Number of Players" heading, a parent is included unless otherwise indicated. By reading the "How to Play" section, you can determine whether the activity is appropriate for your child. The "Hints and Variations" section will provide you with expanded guidelines for play so the games can be modified to fit your family. Personalized variations will add to your enjoyment while improving your child's self-esteem as well as her thinking skills.

Of course, every child is different, but all benefit from attention and validation. It is important to remember that how your child learns can be even more important than what he learns. Focus on the process. Albert Einstein said, "Imagination is more important than knowledge, for knowledge is limited, whereas imagination embraces the entire world." You can create an atmosphere where creative thinking flourishes. It just takes the desire to do so. But because many parents don't have hours to spend, the activities in this book are designed to give the maximum benefit in the minimum amount of time. Some take only minutes to play, require no special materials, and may be taken up at the spur of the moment.

I have also attacked one of the other stumbling blocks to our success in helping our own children. When my children were younger, most of the games they wanted to play were not enjoyable to me as an adult. Most were too repetitive; they did not use thinking skills creatively; they were too long; and someone always felt like a loser. I hated going around the same game board over and over again. So I planned activities that challenged me and the children, with an emphasis on creativity and humor. If I wanted to play with the children, the games would have to be fun for all of us.

These activities teach new skills, enhance old ones, and best of all, don't feel like work. They use basic skills in new and different ways every time each game is played. The reading and writing activities develop language skills that help children make themselves understood. While playing the math games, your child will use math facts not only to arrive at a sum or a remainder, but to make judgments about his immediate world and to arrive at logical conclusions. Because strategy is an important part of all the games, your child will develop strong thinking and problem solving skills.

These games accept the fact that most children enjoy competition, but ensure that the enjoyment of playing is more important than winning or losing. (If a competition is stressful for your child, you don't have to keep score.) Remember, winning does not necessarily mean someone else has to lose. We need to think of winning as the accomplishment of an objective—a goal reached.

The activities allow enough variation in rules so children of different ages can play with parents at the same time. You can encourage your children to use their imaginations and their creativity in picking materials for some of the games or in making variations in the playing style. For children who enjoy playing commercial games, they may even create their own game boards from a shirt cardboard or a file folder. They may add bonus or penalty squares to introduce the element of chance. The choice is theirs.

You will need no special knowledge to play. You don't have to know phonics or algorithms. You need only be open to new ideas. It is important to use your child's knowledge as a base to build on. If your child is just starting to recognize beginning and ending sounds in words, encourage her to play the games that will strengthen those skills. If she has a basic understanding of math facts, but needs some drill work, guide her toward a game that makes strengthening memory skills fun. Be sure to reward creative behavior, and your child will begin to view learning as an exciting and self-rewarding activity.

You can provide a rich environment and a variety of activities to stimulate your child's imagination. Allow your child to be directly involved in choosing the activity and interpreting the rules. Play with your child and show him that learning, at any age, can be fun. You will plant a seed and watch your child grow in self-esteem, curiosity, creativity, and independence.

The games also help alleviate guilt. Sure, we would all like to have the time to pack our children in the car once or twice a week to see the latest exhibit at a science museum, or a children's museum, or an art museum. That's just not always possible. We may not have a lot of time, but we can make the most of the time we have. We can enrich our children's lives in short bursts when we recognize that

that time is important and valuable to a child's development. We can do something at home that is challenging, productive, and creative. Because the activities use materials found around the house (newspapers, cards, kitchen items), the games can begin spontaneously.

These activities don't expect you to be a teacher in the classroom sense. Instead, they help you find ways to interact with your child as a parent who loves her, and wants to enjoy her company. The activities teach that learning never stops, no matter how old you are.

If your child is resistant, don't force the games on him. Try to determine why he does not want to play. Is he afraid he will lose, or is he embarrassed to be playing where his friends might see him? Is he unsure of his ability with words or numbers, or does he just want to be someplace else? All of these issues exist at some time and must be taken into consideration. If you still cannot get him involved, postpone the activity. Try again at the dinner table or at the breakfast table, but don't get upset if he won't take the bait. These games are designed to increase fun times with your child, not to produce tension.

When working with your child on academic skills, you can use the same approach as you would in teaching him a sport. A child learns to pitch a baseball or ride a bike by practicing with his parent. You point out technique, you discuss strategy, you act as a role model, and you praise the child at every opportunity as he gets closer to the goal you both have set. You work toward establishing good habits.

The time you set aside may be as individual as the game you choose to play. It is important to choose a time when you are full of energy and enthusiasm. If you are an evening person, try the time right after dinner. If you are a morning person, you can play parts of these games at the breakfast table or on Saturday morning. But if your best time coincides with your child's favorite cartoon, postpone your game time.

Your child's best learning time must also be taken into consideration. Passive or hostile learners rarely absorb much. It would be ideal if both you and your child have the same high-energy time, but that is rarely the case. My sons were both grouchy in the morning—my best time. They would hardly talk, much less answer questions. It was hard enough to find out what they wanted for lunch! This was not a good time to try to play games. When that happened, I had to be the one to compromise, at least until they were more interested in and enthusiastic about the activities.

In order to get my sons started, I offered an extension of their bedtime with the understanding that the time would be used for us to play a game together. We agreed to complete at least one round. The first time we played a game, I assembled the necessary materials and determined where we would play: the kitchen table. One sat back with his arms crossed over his chest and the other insisted on sitting in my lap. I said a two-word sentence, and they had to add words to make complete sentences. When they finally responded, the sentences were very silly and they made us laugh. The sillier the sentences became, the more involved the boys were. They even forgot to keep score. After the agreed-upon fifteen minutes of play, they wanted to continue; and the next night they asked to play the game again. It had worked!

As they became familiar with the games, they began to choose their favorites, usually the ones they felt they had a good chance of winning. My greatest pleasure came when they began to see the possibilities for play at other times of the day, or when a question from one of the games could be thrown out at any time and everyone would get involved in an abbreviated version of the game.

One of my boys was better at reading and the other was good at math. Sometimes I could get them both to participate if they knew we would have time for both a reading and a math activity. Other times, only one of them would play while the other watched. Each avoided the chance of losing to his brother. This was okay. Fun is usually contagious, and even if they were not pulled into the game, they learned by watching.

All of the games are designed to be open-ended. The "rules" are given as guidelines to play. Feel free to vary the rules and the method of scoring if they do not fit your child or your immediate situation. These games were built on flexibility and can only be enhanced by variation.

Keep in mind that when you play these games with your family, everyone is a winner. As your child grows in confidence and ability, she will develop the creative and critical thinking skills for success in the classroom and at home. Your family will grow closer with each opportunity to share a common activity, one that is specifically designed to be stimulating for both adults and children. Together you're embarking on a special adventure that provides a nurturing combination of love, learning, and laughter. Enjoy!

ONE

WORDS, WORDS, WORDS

Helping Your Child Develop Reading Skills

When we help our children develop reading skills, we give them one of the greatest gifts—a facility with language. Not only will they have the ability to learn, to recall, and to share information, which is useful and important in the classroom, but they will develop a sense of self-esteem that they will carry with them through their school years and into their adult lives. Children with strong verbal skills and a solid foundation in reading are ready to succeed in the classroom, and that success will prepare them for the increasingly complex world in which we live.

Research indicates that the early school years are the most formative in a child's learning; 80 percent of a child's measurable intelligence is developed by the age of eight. We know, too, that this is the time when children grow in their self-esteem, cultural identity, independence, and ability to deal with the world around them. It is also a time when they need to develop a fascination with learning and with words. They must learn to manipulate written and spoken language, that is, to read and write, if they are to master their world and become independent adults. And the process must begin when they are very young.

Imagine yourself in a foreign country. Let's say someplace in the Orient. You do not understand the language. Not only are you unable to read the signs, you don't even recognize the letters of the alphabet. How would you survive?

The situation is not that different for your very young child. But eventually, she recognizes your words and learns to mimic them. With time, her mimicry begins to have meaning. You read to her and she realizes that the printed word has meaning, too. As she learns to read, to write, and to think clearly, her communication skills become a strength. The ability to make herself understood gives her confidence.

You probably recognize that a child's self-esteem can be enhanced or destroyed on the athletic field. You know that successful opportunities to perform dramatically or musically can make a difference. But in the early elementary years a child's self-esteem is just as often tied into her ability to read. Many schools group children by ability level for reading instruction. Whether they call these reading groups remedial through advanced, the reds and the blues, or by titles of their reading texts, children know whether they are achieving at the top or at the bottom of the class.

A child with a reading disability told me that he thought the reason he needed special help with his reading in social studies was because he was not as smart as the other kids. When I suggest that many of our most intelligent scientists had some difficulty with reading in their early years, he was shocked. Few realize Albert Einstein was not able to speak until he was four years old and was seven before he could read. Thomas Edison was told by his teachers that he was too stupid to learn anything.

Teachers today are much more sensitive to learning styles and to developmental levels. They adjust their teaching to accommodate children who learn better when taught to read by learning the letter sounds. They realize that some children need to be taught to read with a sight approach—remembering words by how they look. They know that not all children are ready to read at the same time and they try to help each child develop at her own rate.

But, as parents, we should also keep a watchful eye to ensure that our children do not suffer in their sense of self because of difficulties in reading. Many children do not learn the mechanics of reading until after the first grade, whereas some learn them before kindergarten. Although adults know that children acquire skills at different rates, the comparisons the children make among themselves and their peers often make them feel inferior. When we take time to play developmental games with our children, we can show them that we have faith in their abilities. As parents, we should let them know that we believe in them as learners and readers, no matter where they fall in their classroom placement.

The government study *What Works* states, "Children improve their reading ability by reading a lot. Reading achievement is directly related to the amount of reading children do in school and outside."

Most of us know that practice makes perfect, yet the study also found that in the average elementary school, children spend 7 to 8 minutes a day reading silently. That's not a lot of practice time. Half the fifth graders spend 4 minutes a day reading, but spend an average of 130 minutes watching television. We want to change that. If we want our children to be as excited about reading as they are about television, we have to feel that excitement ourselves. We have to enjoy reading and share that joy with our children. We must also accept that we are competing for their time with a very exciting medium. We need to make reading activities as much fun as watching turtles. The games in this section are fun and exciting, and they are educational. Your children will be having fun and probably won't even realize they are developing their thinking skills at the same time.

You can begin by helping your child improve her ability to read and to understand what she is reading. You can help her recall specific facts, and more important, you can help her to that next level of reading, the ability to draw conclusions based on what she has read. If your child reads about termites, she will probably read that they are small creatures capable of doing major damage to wooden structures. You want your child to take that information to the next step and understand or assume that you would call an exterminator if you found them in your house. When she reads about dolphins, you want her to remember the specific information she read, but you also want her to begin to understand why environmental groups are working so hard to save these animals.

Schools do, of course, work on comprehension skills and place much emphasis on the "WH" questions: who, what, when, where, why. The who, what, when, and where questions involve memory and the ability to recall, but our children also need to learn to develop the skills to answer the why questions in order to analyze and generalize—to apply what they have learned to their own lives.

Your child probably knows the story "Little Red Riding Hood." I'm sure she can tell you the main characters, the who of the book. She can probably tell you where Little Red Riding Hood was going, what she was wearing, and probably even the time of day. But begin asking the why questions, and many children begin to be less confident.

Why did the wolf choose Red as his victim? Was he attracted by her cape? What is the message or the moral of the story? Don't visit your grandmother?

And this is just a simple fairy tale. What happens when children begin reading more complex material? Will they have the thinking skills to understand more than the basic details? In a relaxed home setting, and with you as a guide, your child will have the time and the encouragement to practice the thinking skills she will need as the work gets more difficult.

We want our children to be readers, and we can encourage them to read. We want them to develop sophisticated thinking skills, and we can encourage them to think. We want them to feel successful, and we can provide opportunities for that success. With the activities in this section, we can help them develop their reading and thinking skills as well as their confidence.

The games in this section provide your children with positive experiences with the written word, with reading, and with books. They are not intended to teach the mechanics of reading. That is the job of the school. What these games will do is encourage your child to want to read, and they will help her read creatively and productively, improving her comprehension skills.

For the preschool and kindergarten child, the exercises will concentrate on the pre-reading skills that a child needs in order to learn to read and to understand the meaning of words. For the older child who can already identify words, the emphasis will be on helping her think about what she is reading. The game encourages children to detect the main idea. They provide opportunities for comparing and contrasting and for examining cause and effect. The games teach children to classify and interpret information and help them make judgments, including books, magazines, and maps, which will help your child develop solid research skills. But, best of all, your child will be spending enjoyable time with you.

Although these games help develop reading and verbal skills, I strongly encourage you also to spend at least part of every day reading aloud to your child. A period of reading time set aside each day will help your child develop not only the skills needed for reading success, but a joy of language that you can share while snuggled in a favorite chair or curled up in bed.

Because children's listening skills are usually more advanced than their reading abilities, when you read to your child, you share information well above her reading level.

The following games will enhance your read-aloud sessions. Although the skills developed with these games are serious skills, the games are not. These are not classroom activities. Giggling, laughing, and generous applause are encouraged. Have fun!

BEGINNINGS

PURPOSE: This game helps your child learn beginning sounds and helps him learn to sound out words. It also builds vocabulary.

MATERIALS NEEDED: No materials are needed to play this game, so it can be played anywhere, at any time. Use it any time you can—cooking dinner, riding in a car, waiting in a restaurant, walking down the street.

NUMBER OF PLAYERS: 2 to 6.

TIME: Each turn takes under 5 minutes, so this is a good spur-of-the-moment activity.

SKILLS DEVELOPED: The ability to group words by the beginning sound is one method of categorizing and organizing information. It provides a framework for logical thinking. "Beginnings" requires your child to identify words by their beginning sound—for example, words that begin with a hard C—and to group them with other words that begin with the same sound—such as *cat, car, caterpillar*. Because there is no written component to this game, it will encourage your child to be more attentive to his environment and will help him build a longer attention span. Both of these skills are needed throughout school years and in almost any job situation. Both a secretary and a scientist must pay attention to what is going on around them and must give their complete attention to their work.

HOW TO PLAY: The object of this game is for players to find objects that begin with the same sound. One player chooses a letter sound or letter blend sound (*sh, bl, gr, sk, sm, sp,* and so on) and announces it to the group. Each player, in turn, names something in the immediate area that begins with that letter or blend sound. The winner is the last one to find an object with the selected beginning sound. For example, while walking down the street, the first player chooses the blend *sh* and says *shoe*. The next player says *shorts*. The next says *shovel*. Play continues until no player is able to see an object that begins with *sh*. At that point the round is over and the person who named the last object is the winner.

HINTS AND VARIATIONS: Instead of finding the objects in the area, the players can also develop vocabulary by simply naming any word they can think of that begins with the beginning sound.

Another variation would be for the first player to begin by selecting an object in the area and revealing only the beginning sound, for example *b*. The other players must guess the secret object. The first player to guess the object is the winner. If the players are having a difficult time discovering the object, they may ask yes and no questions in order to determine its location and use. Examples: *Is someone wearing it? Is it on the wall? Can I hold it in my hand?* This is a great time to reward creativity and imagination.

One of my favorite examples was my son's choice of my contact lens for the beginning sound *l*.

RHYME TIME

PURPOSE: With this game, your child will build skills in sounding out words by practicing ending sounds. The game will also build vocabulary.

MATERIALS NEEDED: No materials are needed to play this game, so it can be played anywhere. Play while waiting for a doctor's appointment or for a waitress in a restaurant.

NUMBER OF PLAYERS: 2 to 6.

TIME: Each turn takes under 5 minutes and can be played any time you are together with children and nothing else is going on.

SKILLS DEVELOPED: As she learns to read, your child needs to be able to know how to rhyme in order to be able to sound out unfamiliar words. Once she knows that the combination of *a* and *t* makes the sound *at*, she can sound out words such as *cat, bat, rat,* and so on. We use this skill throughout our lives as we are always seeing words we do not know. One of the methods we use to pronounce unfamiliar words is to break them down by syllable and look for familiar rhyming patterns. It provides an additional framework for attacking the unknown. *Bequeath* could be a very difficult word if we didn't already know the word *beneath.*

This activity encourages your child to become more alert to her environment, because she needs to look for objects that fit the rhyming sequence of the game. She will begin to see new relationships between words and will understand and apply the rules of rhyming.

HOW TO PLAY: The object of this game is for players to come up with words that rhyme with a clue word. Players take turns naming the clue word, one that has rhyming possibilities. Each player, in turn, names another word that rhymes with the clue word. For example, with the word *bear,* players might say *wear, tear, fair, care, share, stare* and *mare.* If one player is unable to answer, she can forfeit her turn and the next player can respond. If the play continues around, the player who forfeited will be given another chance. The last player to name a rhyming word chooses the clue word for the next round.

HINTS AND VARIATIONS: This is a particularly good game for your younger child. Since preschools and kindergartens spend a lot of time with rhyming, it will give her a chance to show off at home what she has learned at school, and will ease the frustrations she may feel with the more difficult games older siblings might like to play. Success at these early level games builds confidence and can improve self-esteem.

FUNNY PAPER FUN

PURPOSE: This game helps develop skills in comprehension, sequencing (putting things in their proper order), and cause and effect.

MATERIALS NEEDED: You will need the comic strips from the newspaper, scissors, and pencils for this game.

NUMBER OF PLAYERS: 2 (This game can be played with more players if you have more than one child, but I like to use this game in a one-to-one environment to give the child a little undivided attention.)

TIME: Allow at least 15 minutes for one round. If you have more time, each player can present more than one comic strip.

SKILLS DEVELOPED: In order for your child to understand what he reads, he must understand what happens first, second, third, and so on. He has to see how events happen in a logical order and that one event can cause another. This is particularly important in social studies and in reading biographies. When memorizing history facts, your child must know that the Revolutionary War came *before* the Civil War, and *after* the pilgrims landed at Plymouth Rock. By using comic strips to develop this sequencing skill, your child is able to use his own language to make sense of the events of the story presented in the strip.

HOW TO PLAY: The object of this game is for players to successfully rearrange scrambled comic strips. Use the comic pages of a newspaper, children's magazine, or commercial comic book. Each player chooses a favorite comic strip. Your rebel might choose "Calvin and Hobbes." A sensitivity specialist might choose "Peanuts." Cat lovers would probably choose "Garfield." The player numbers the back of each panel of the strip in order (1, 2, 3, 4), cuts the strip into sections, and scrambles the pieces. Pencils are best for this activity as the ink of pens shows through the other side. The players trade strips. Each player arranges the pieces of the other player's strip in correct order. The first to finish unscrambling correctly wins.

HINTS AND VARIATIONS: When played for more than one round, it is possible to allow a little more variety and creativity to the game. The player who comes up with the correct sequence of the strip could be awarded 5 points, but if your child is able to come up with a story that justifies a different sequence of the strip's pieces, he should be awarded bonus points.

    If you are using the newspaper, save the comics for a few days in order to offer more choices.

Let the preschooler (or nonreader) tell you what he thinks is happening in the cartoon and make up a story to go with the pictures. Preschoolers look at events so differently than we do and their versions often create enjoyable variations. Young children love telling stories and parents love hearing them. What could be more fun?

THE SAME GAME

PURPOSE: This game helps your child categorize information and encourages vocabulary development.

MATERIALS NEEDED: This activity does not involve any materials and is a good one to play in a car or while waiting.

NUMBER OF PLAYERS: Minimum of 2, but can be played in teams of up to 10.

TIME: Each round could take 5 minutes or more, depending on the level of difficulty. Save this one for when you have a long stretch of uninterrupted time.

SKILLS DEVELOPED: Children need to understand that words can have more than one meaning. Successful education requires flexible thinking, and the ability to do well on standardized tests depends on it. Your child must be aware that many words have more than one meaning and can fit into more than one category. The word *light* can refer to weight, the opposite of dark, or fewer calories or reduced fat. It is difficult for her to get a real understanding of a word she reads unless she is able to see how the context of the passage gives the word meaning.

HOW TO PLAY: Here, players guess the category that a group of words fits into. One player thinks of a category (for example, *sharp things*), which she does not reveal, and then names an object that belongs to that category (for example, *knife*). The other players must try to guess the secret category. The original player names additional objects that belong in the same category—*razor,* then *pencil point,* and so on—until one of the players can guess the correct category. If no one is able to guess the category (or come close), the original player wins the point and the right to another turn.

HINTS AND VARIATIONS: This activity might be more difficult for younger children, so rather than making it an individual effort, you might divide the players into teams. With this and other more difficult activities, be sure to give points for sense of humor and a friendly, cooperative manner. Some suggestions for possible categories include *color, hot things, cold things, heavy things, silly things.* Have fun.

PREDICTIONS

PURPOSE: "Predictions" encourages your child to look for patterns in his reading material and to be a keen observer of what he sees around him in the world. It also helps develop study skills.

MATERIALS NEEDED: No materials are needed, but this game should be played in a place of activity or changing environment, such as in a car, restaurant, or other public place.

NUMBER OF PLAYERS: Minimum of 2, maximum, a car full.

TIME: Each turn could take 5 minutes or more. "Predictions" is good for a long car trip.

SKILLS DEVELOPED: The ability to sense cause and effect and to anticipate consequences is important for higher levels of reading comprehension. In order to be an active reader, your child will need to question what he reads and make predictions about the events before he finishes the material. He needs to think about what he is reading and see if it makes sense. When children question and anticipate as they read, they strengthen their comprehension skills.

HOW TO PLAY: The object of the game is for players to predict what will happen next. Each player, in turn, poses a question relevant to the environment. For example, in a car, he might ask how many blue cars will pass before a yellow one does. In a restaurant, your child might ask how quickly your water glasses will be refilled after you empty them. All players make their predictions and then watch to see what actually happens. The player who comes closest to the actual result is the winner.

HINTS AND VARIATIONS: To make the play faster and more fun, all players can pose their questions at the same time, so they are waiting and watching for more than one event. Other examples of possible questions are: "Who will be taken next at the doctor's office?" "Which car will try to change lanes first in a traffic jam?" "Which table will receive its food first?"

The one my boys liked best was, "How soon will Dad lose his temper when the driver in front of him is going too slowly?"

PICKA

PURPOSE: While improving her reading vocabulary, your child improves her powers of observation and develops categorization skills with this game.

MATERIALS NEEDED: There are no specific materials needed. This game can be played at home, in the car, or while waiting in a restaurant or for an office appointment. It provides a constructive use of time that might otherwise be wasted in boredom.

NUMBER OF PLAYERS: 2 to 6.

TIME: Each turn takes under 5 minutes, so you can play for as long or as short a time as you have available.

SKILLS DEVELOPED: Your child needs to understand similarities and differences in concrete items as well as abstract ideas. A table and a chair are both pieces of furniture, but they have different uses. Love and hate are both emotions, but they have very different expressions. She needs to be able to identify words by their relationship to other words and to be able to group words into categories.

This game requires each player to choose a category for her turn and to be able to provide words that are examples of that category. She might have to use her imagination and powers of persuasion to prove a word she chooses belongs in a particular category. (If she can support the ideas that *Santa Claus* fits into the *round* category, let her do so.) Your child will develop planning strategies when selecting a category. With practice, she will learn to choose a broad category such as *sports,* rather than a very limited category such as words that *rhyme with oranges.*

HOW TO PLAY: The object of the game is to be the last person to provide a word that fits into a particular category. Each player, in turn, chooses a category and tells it to the other players. For example, *round, yellow* and *wooden* could be categories. Then each player, including the one who chose the category, names something she sees that fits into the category. Choices in the *round* category might be: *table, coins, plates, eyes.* The winner is the last person who can name something to fit into the category.

The next person chooses another category and play continues until the time you've allowed for the game is over, or until dinner arrives.

HINTS AND VARIATIONS: The complexity of the categories needs to be tailored to the ages of the children. When playing with older children, you could use more abstract ideas for categories, such as *boring (a yawn, unappetizing food, conversation); clinging (clothes, drapes, people); empty (glass, mind, hunger).* Do not limit creativity in the choice of a category, as that is a major component of the game. When playing in public places, you can teach your child the concept of tact. The waitress should not be included in the *round* or *ugly* category if she can hear the answers! Always feel free to help the child think of categories if she is stuck by providing clues: "What about a color?" "What about a shape?"

As this game is the reverse of "The Same Game," you might want to use these two games interchangeably. In "The Same Game," your child must take specific clues and find their broad category. In "Picka," she must find words that fit into a known category.

LOCATION PLEASE

PURPOSE: This game gives your child a better sense of the world and his place in it, while it helps him improve his map-reading skills.

MATERIALS NEEDED: For this game you will need a map, an atlas, or a globe. For younger children, you should begin with a large map of one state and progress to maps of countries and continents as the child gains proficiency in map skills. (See Hints and Variations. A game board and dice will be needed if played as suggested there.)

NUMBER OF PLAYERS: 2 to 6.

TIME: Each round will take from 5 to 10 minutes. Play as many rounds as you have time for.

SKILLS DEVELOPED: Reading is not limited to words. A child also needs to be able to obtain information from charts, graphs, and maps. Throughout school, he will be exposed to maps in social studies and in geography. He will need to be able to locate cities, rivers, and countries and to understand their relationships to each other. Maps are an important source of information about our ever-changing world. This activity provides a fun way to work with a map and will encourage your child to see the location of an area within the framework of a larger geographical sphere. A better understanding of world geography fosters a clearer understanding of world events and how they affect us.

HOW TO PLAY: The object of this game is to be the first one to discover a secret location on a map. Taking turns, each player chooses a secret place in an atlas, on the map, or on the globe. The secret location can be as precise as Central Park on a map of New York, or as general as the Atlantic Ocean on a globe. The other players ask yes/no questions to obtain information about the location. For example, using the map of the United States, the secret location might be Boston. Possible questions would include: "Are you a city?" "Are you in New England?" "Are you in Massachusetts?" The first player to guess the correct location gets a point. The player with the most points at the end of the available time wins.

HINTS AND VARIATIONS: It's also fun to play this game with a game board. The first player to guess the correct location rolls the dice and moves around the board. If you construct your own game board, why not make a city in the home spot? Rivers, oceans, mountains, and the like could be included on the game board. Penalty squares and bonus squares—such as *lose one turn* or *move two extra spaces*—might also be included. Many elementary school children do not fully understand the meaning of *state, city, country*. You can use this activity to help them come to a better understanding of these terms.

I have even played using a map of our town, which helped my son get to his friends' house on his bike.

BOGUS

PURPOSE: This game helps your child become more familiar with using a dictionary and makes her more aware of the multiple meanings of words.

MATERIALS NEEDED: For this game you will need a dictionary. Be sure to use a dictionary that is appropriate to the reading level of your child. Many dictionaries are available in picture versions. You will also need a game board, markers, and dice. You can use a commercial game board from another game or create your own. You could also use the outside squares of a checkerboard.

NUMBER OF PLAYERS: 2 or more players and an adult supervisor.

TIME: Allow at least 30 minutes to complete your way around the game board.

SKILLS DEVELOPED: Your child will need to be able to use a dictionary throughout her years in school. After she graduates, there are many jobs that require the continued use of a dictionary, including teaching, secretarial positions, writing, and editorial work. The dictionary is usually the first reference children use. By helping develop your child's ability to use one, you will be helping her build the skills she will need later in order to use the encyclopedia and more advanced reference materials.

In her effort to come up with obscure words to present, she will broaden her own vocabulary. Young children enjoy making up meanings for words, and this will provide them with a creative outlet. Remind your child that it is important to keep a straight face when giving a bogus answer.

HOW TO PLAY: The object of the game is to guess the correct meaning for a word when the actual meaning and a fabricated meaning are given. Players roll a die to determine who goes first. Play rotates. The first player chooses a word from the dictionary and presents both the actual definition and a definition she has invented. For example, the word chosen might be *bogus*. The actual definition might be *not genuine*. A fabricated definition might be *a tropical moss*. A more advanced player might use a word such as *terminate* as the chosen word.

The next player must guess the correct definition. If the guess is correct, she rolls the die and moves the number of spaces indicated. If she is incorrect, the player who presented the definition rolls and moves. The first to circle the board wins.

HINTS AND VARIATIONS: This game works better if the players are close in age and if you act as helper to both of them. It would be difficult for them to stump you with a bogus definition. If you create your own game board, you can include bonus squares such as *roll again* or penalty squares such as *move back two spaces* to add even more of the element of chance to the game.

FIND IT

PURPOSE: This game is designed to give your child practice using reference books to find information and will make him aware of the kinds of reference materials available.

MATERIALS NEEDED: A dictionary, encyclopedia, thesaurus, or atlas, and a timer.

NUMBER OF PLAYERS: 2 to 4.

TIME: Each turn might take 5 to 10 minutes, depending on the reference book used. Finding information in an encyclopedia will take longer than finding it in a dictionary.

SKILLS DEVELOPED: Research skills can help us all find the answers to questions. Many children are not even aware of reference materials and do not realize they have the ability to find the information they need. Your child needs to know that no one is expected to know everything. The ability to use these resources will help him know when, how, and where to seek help. It will also help him become more of an independent learner and will allow him to broaden his knowledge.

HOW TO PLAY: The object of the game is to locate the answer to a specific question by finding the answer in a dictionary, encyclopedia, thesaurus, or atlas. Each player, in turn, asks a question that can only be answered by finding information in a reference book. If your child has difficulty formulating a question, let him skim through the reference book for ideas. The next player is given a time limit in which to find the answer. If he is able to find the answer, he wins that round. If he cannot locate the information, the player who asked the question must be able to show the answer in the reference book, and he is the winner. Allow 5 minutes for questions that use a dictionary or thesaurus and 10 minutes for questions that need an encyclopedia or atlas. Older children should be expected to find answers to specific questions, such as, "How many people live in our state?" Preschoolers might be asked to find the page with the information about airplanes in a picture dictionary.

HINTS AND VARIATIONS: Many excellent reference books are now available in paperback and many others are available at the library. If you can't check these books out of your library, you could play the game in their children's room. Look for books that contain mostly pictures for your preschoolers. If children of different ages and ability levels are playing, use different sets of reference books and make sure you oversee the questions asked to make sure your younger child has a chance to find the answer. You could form teams with the children or two children could team up against you. To make the game go faster, all players can pose questions at the same time, and the person to find the answer first is the winner.

DETAILS

PURPOSE: This game encourages your child to listen carefully and to pay attention to details.

MATERIALS NEEDED: You will need books or magazine articles for this game. Have a variety available so your child will be able to choose. Make sure the books or articles are about subjects she enjoys or ones you would like her to enjoy, but let her choose.

NUMBER OF PLAYERS: Best played with 2, but can be played with an additional child as well.

TIME: You should allow at least 15 minute to get the full enjoyment of this game. That will give you and your child time for one turn each. If you can play longer, you will be able to have more than one turn.

SKILLS DEVELOPED: The most important reading activity a parent can do with a child, no matter what age, is to read aloud to her. This can expose her to materials well above her actual reading level. Most children have a more developed listening comprehension than their reading comprehension. In addition to providing a quiet time for interaction, this activity gives your child some control by allowing her to choose the book herself. This activity can be used with all children, no matter what their reading ability, since you will be doing all of the reading.

HOW TO PLAY: The object of the game is to remember as many details as possible based on the information that is presented. Have your child choose the book to be read. You read a passage from the book that contains a complete idea and ask your child how many details she can restate from what was read. She will receive a point for each detail remembered. Next, your child will tell a story and ask *you* for details. She then decides if you answered correctly and how many points you earn. The winner is the player with the most points at the end of all turns.

HINTS AND VARIATIONS: This might be a good way to get your child to tell you about her day in school. We all are too familiar with the "Nothing" response when we ask our child what happened during the school day. When she is challenging you to remember details, her stories must become more elaborate.

While playing this game with my son, I finally discovered why he came home each day with holes in the knees of his jeans. Instead of simply saying, "I fell," he gave me a detailed description of the daily cannonball games (a form of dodgeball) played at recess.

If you are playing with more than one child, you can give each child a turn to choose the book and answer the questions. If there is a big age difference between the children, you can set the rule ahead of time that you might be giving hints to help the younger child remember details. Be as lenient as possible in your scoring. You want to make sure your child will want to play again. If your child can and wants to read, let her read a passage from her schoolbook when it is her turn to present. This is a good way to get her to do her homework and will help her remember what she has read.

SYNONYMS

PURPOSE: This game helps your child understand how to use a thesaurus and how to practice using words with similar meanings.

MATERIALS NEEDED: You will need a thesaurus for this game. If you cannot find an appropriate thesaurus, use a child's dictionary. The definitions are usually short and more like synonyms than in a regular dictionary. Public libraries usually have circulation copies of these. You will also need a game board. Take one from any commercial game or construct your own with cardboard and markers.

NUMBER OF PLAYERS: The more the merrier.

TIME: Allow 20 minutes or more.

SKILLS DEVELOPED: The ability to find an answer from the appropriate source is often as important as knowing the answer. Your child needs to be comfortable using a thesaurus because it is a skill he will use throughout his school years. As he begins to do more creative writing, he will need to be able to find words to give the proper meaning to what he writes. When he knows that the words are available to him in a book, creative writing becomes an easier task. This game develops reading skills that can then be put to use when writing.

HOW TO PLAY: Explain to your child that *synonyms* are words that have the same or similar meanings. You can explain how words mean the same thing by giving examples, *big/large, tiny/small, bucket/pail.* The object of the game is to give as many words as possible that mean the same thing as the clue word. It can be played in two ways. When playing with young children, you choose a word from the thesaurus and ask for a synonym. Each player gives one synonym in turn and moves his marker one space on the game board until the ideas are exhausted. For example, if the clue word is *sport,* the synonyms would be *game, hobby, contest, fun, play.* Then a new word is chosen and the procedure is repeated. The last to give a correct guess gets a bonus move. The first player to make a complete circle of the board is the winner.

Older children can play for points. Play rotates. Each player, in turn, chooses a word from the thesaurus. All players, including the one who chose the word, list as many synonyms as they can think of on a piece of paper. Players read their lists aloud and cross off any words that were listed by any other player. Score one point for each correct guess that no one else has chosen. The player with the most points at the end of the allotted time is the winner. For each round, allow 3 to 5 minutes to complete the lists.

HINTS AND VARIATIONS: This game requires abstract thinking and might not be appropriate for the very young child. It is a good game to play with your child and his friends as it works better with more players. The use of a game board makes it more like a commercial game and that appeals to many children.

WORD HUNT

PURPOSE: This game helps your child to develop her skills in categorization.

MATERIALS NEEDED: Children's magazines. *Weekly Reader* is a good choice and most schools allow children to bring them home. Colored pencils or pens are optional.

NUMBER OF PLAYERS: 2 to 4.

TIME: Each round should take approximately 10 minutes.

SKILLS DEVELOPED: The ability to skim and locate a particular word or concept is an important study skill that is used throughout school and into adult life. Many jobs, including those in education, business, and journalism, require the ability to skim in order to retrieve information in the shortest possible time.

Since your child will be expected to label words as either nouns (people, places, or things), verbs (action words), or adjectives and adverbs (describing words), she will become more aware of the multiple uses of some words. The word *move* might be a noun when it is *the* move from one house to another, or it might be a verb when you move your checker in a checkers game.

Your child can also use this exercise to increase her vocabulary, because she will be exposed to the words you have identified in your reading passage that she might not have known.

HOW TO PLAY: The object of the game is to find all the nouns, verbs, or adjectives and adverbs within a reading selection. Each player chooses an article from a children's magazine. If you are participating, use a regular magazine or a newspaper for your selection. Each player chooses a particular category. Since your child may not know the terms *noun, verb, adjective and adverb,* use category designations she will understand. If you are searching for nouns, make the category *people, places, things.* If you are searching for verbs, call the category *action words.* When searching for adjectives or adverbs, the category might be called *words that describe things.*

Once the category is determined, each player searches her article and circles all the words that fit into that category. Players then read their words aloud and the player (or players) who has circled all the correct words within the time limit wins.

In order to even the odds, you might have a shorter time limit to read your own passage since your skimming skills are probably faster than your child's! An example of selections in the *people, places, things* category in a sentence about Coca-Cola would be: *COCA-COLA is a DRINK that has become unusually popular in AMERICA and throughout the WORLD.*

HINTS AND VARIATIONS: If you use a different colored pen for each category, you can use the same article more than one time.

Before beginning the activity, you might need to help your child read through the article to help her understand what she is reading. To play with a preschooler, use comic strips and have the child identify pictures that fit into the categories. In that case, you might want to call the categories *people; things; colors;* or *what people are doing.*

SOMETHING'S MISSING

PURPOSE: This game requires your child to draw on what he has learned in the past about a specific topic as he reads new material.

MATERIALS NEEDED: Children's magazines (not borrowed), paper and pencils, and a laundry or magic marker.

NUMBER OF PLAYERS: Works best with 2 players or 2 teams of players.

TIME: At least 30 minutes.

SKILLS DEVELOPED: Much of what your child learns in school is built upon previous learning. The child's common question "Why do I need to know that?" is often answered with reference to future courses of studies, but the future seems so far away that the answer has little meaning for him. He needs to understand that all learning, no matter how trivial it appears, is important in building a framework for future exploration. He needs to see that the future can be as close as tomorrow or five minutes from now, and that it will be necessary for him to apply what he has learned to new situations. What we read has meaning to us because of things we have already learned. When a child reads that a sailor is lost at sea, he knows the sailor is surrounded by water, but will have nothing to drink. The child has previously learned that the ocean contains salt water and humans cannot drink it.

In order to guess the missing words in this activity, he will need to draw on information he has already learned about the subject presented. This task needs to be approached in a methodical and orderly fashion and encourages logical as well as abstract and creative thinking.

HOW TO PLAY: The object of the game is to guess the words that are missing from a sentence by using the context of the sentence for clues. Each player chooses a sentence from a different child's magazine article and copies two or three words from the sentence of a piece of paper, which he keeps hidden. Players then use a marker to eliminate those words from the text. Each player announces the subject of his article and then trades his sentence for the other player's or other team's sentence. Each player examines the sentence and tries to figure out the missing words based on what he knows about the subject. For example, a sentence from an article about food might be, "Plants, animals, and people must have food in order to grow and to keep healthy." The words *animals, food,* and *healthy* might be marked out and the other player would have to try to guess what they are. Don't take out all important words because there would be no context left to help with guesses. The player or team gets 1 point for each correct guess and the player or team with the most points wins.

HINTS AND VARIATIONS: If a particular task appears to be confusing for the child, make sure you take the first turn. The child will learn how to use the context of the sentence by watching the way you do it. You can orally go through the steps you are taking so that the child will have some idea of how to approach the task. You would read the sentence aloud saying the word *blank* at each missing word, and play around with a few words to see if any of them make sense in that place. If you are playing with a preschooler, you will want to team up with the child and let him help you fill in the blanks with information you provide orally.

A variation of this game would allow you to give points for answers other than the correct ones if the child uses the correct type of word (noun, verb), and creates a sentence with a high degree of originality and humor (i.e. points for the creative process).

GOT IT!

PURPOSE: This game helps your child learn how to skim through written material to find important information.

MATERIALS NEEDED: You will need children's magazines for this game. This is a good way for you to encourage your child to read all of those magazines you subscribe to for her but she never seems to open.

NUMBER OF PLAYERS: 2 to 4.

TIME: Allow at least 30 minutes for this game to allow time for several rounds.

SKILLS DEVELOPED: Skimming skills are important when studying for exams or quizzes, working on reports, and taking standardized tests. Even as adults, when we need to be able to get information fast we skim an article or recipe for the main points or ingredients. Your child needs to learn that there is more than one way to get information from books and that it is appropriate to take this shortcut in some situations.

When your child's book report is due the following day and she hasn't even started reading "Little House on the Prairie," it is essential that she know how to skim. If you haven't yet had this wonderful experience, just wait!

HOW TO PLAY: The object of this game is to find specific information from an article by skimming. Each participant chooses the article she will read from a children's magazine. The articles used by the players should be of approximately the same length. At the beginning of each round, one player announces whether the players will be expected to find *who* or *what* the article is about, *where* it took place, or *when* it happened. Each player takes a turn choosing the category. The winner is the first to find the answer to the question in her article and to call out "Got it." In case of a tie, bonus points could be awarded for answers to a "Why did it happen?" or "How did it happen?" question.

If you are playing with a preschooler, you might read the passage to your child and have her answer the questions. Although this will not develop skimming skills, it will develop listening skills and vocabulary. You can use the same article for more than one round of this game as the information you will be seeking will be different each time.

HINTS AND VARIATIONS: Many articles do not provide all the information players might call for and expectations would have to be adjusted accordingly. You could also play this game with your child using her homework assignment while you use a magazine you have not had time to read. Use any opportunity to incorporate homework in a relaxed atmosphere.

DO YOU KNOW?

PURPOSE: This game requires your child to draw conclusions from information he has learned at school or at home and helps improve his vocabulary.

MATERIALS NEEDED: Newspapers or magazines (may be borrowed), pencils and paper, and a dictionary.

NUMBER OF PLAYERS: This game is better if it is played by 2 or more children with you as the moderator and helper, because it will be difficult for your child to find vocabulary you do not know.

TIME: Allow 15 minutes for each round.

SKILLS DEVELOPED: Your child needs to be aware of the vocabulary that is specific to a particular topic in order to more fully understand the topic. In reading about cowboys it helps to be familiar with words such as *lariat, herds,* and *branding.* This game forces him to look at the context and vocabulary of an article and try to guess the meaning of a word from the information he knows about a subject. He must understand that words create a picture of a complete idea. He will be choosing words for his opponents that he hopes they will not know. In doing so, he will be stretching his vocabulary. When it is his turn to give meanings for his opponent's words, he will have to clearly state his definitions. The way he uses language to form a complete thought will be important here.

HOW TO PLAY: The object of this game is to be able to guess the meaning of words given by another player. Using separate newspaper or magazine articles, players choose five words that the other players may not know about a particular topic. The players write their words on a slip of paper. Each player, in turn, presents aloud the topic of his article and his words. The other players, in turn, get a chance to define each word until someone is successful or until they all give up. The presenting player gets 1 point for each word that cannot be defined by the other players. The players providing the definitions receive 1 point for each word that is correctly defined. The player with the most points at the end of the round is the winner.

HINTS AND VARIATIONS: You may need a dictionary to verify definitions in case of a dispute. Disputes are very helpful in games like these, because they encourage each child to defend his choices by using many different language skills to persuade and convince. You might be cultivating a debater or a future politician.

When I played this game with my sons, they enjoyed stumping me with their knowledge of sports terms.

An interesting variation might be for each player to give the words to be defined to the other players, but *not* the article topic. The other players not only have to define the words, but must also guess the topic of the article.

CATEGORIES

PURPOSE: This game helps your child with her skimming and categorizing skills and provides practice in charting information.

MATERIALS NEEDED: Children's magazines, paper, and pencils.

NUMBER OF PLAYERS: 2 to 4.

TIME: Allow 30 minutes.

SKILLS DEVELOPED: Getting information by reading charts is an important skill to develop. Your child will have a better idea of how to read charts if she has the opportunity to create her own. She must provide examples of items that fit into a particular category and she will need to place them into spaces on a chart. This will provide practice in grouping words by category. The more she understands about particular words or ideas, the more meaning she will be able to get from what she reads. If she knows that Chris Evert is a wife, an athlete, and a wage earner, she will have a better understanding of the total person.

HOW TO PLAY: The object of the game is to locate words to fill the category spaces on a chart. Each player enters three agreed upon category topics at the top of her page and chooses a four to six letter name found in a children's magazine article and writes it down the side of her page. For example:

	PEOPLE	PLACES	THINGS
B			
U			
S			
H			

Each player must fill in the columns on her chart with words that begin with the letter at the left side and that fit the category. The name and all category words must come from her chosen magazine article. Points are given for each word placed correctly in a given time limit and the player with the most points wins. You will want to decide how much time to allow for each round depending on how successful the players are. If you feel your child wants to spend more time on each round, encourage her to do so. Other categories you could use at the top of the page are *actions, describing words, animals,* or anything else agreed upon by the players. It may not be possible to fill all the spaces. For example, in an article about tennis, players might find:

	PEOPLE	PLACES	THINGS
M	McEnroe	Melbourne	Money
O			overhead
N		New York	net
I	Ivan		ice
C	Coach	clubhouse	callus
A	Ashe		

HINTS AND VARIATIONS: If you are playing alone with a child, you could use a more difficult magazine to complete your portion. Keep in mind that adults can write much more quickly than children, so take your time. If you are playing with a preschooler, you will want to form teams. You can read the word for the child and ask her to place it in the proper category.

OPPOSITES

PURPOSE: This game helps your child understand the language of opposites and develops imagination skills.

MATERIALS NEEDED: No materials are needed, but this game needs to be played in a place with a lot of activity. It provides a fun way to divert young children during a long wait in a restaurant or on a long car ride, and creates a positive interaction in a situation that could easily be negative.

NUMBER OF PLAYERS: 2 to 4.

TIME: Allow 5 minutes for each round.

SKILLS DEVELOPED: Your child will develop a better understanding of the concept of opposites as he begins to understand that a single object can be described with contrasting words. While playing this game, your child will choose an opposite category, for example, *empty/full*. Then, he will search for an item that could be described in the abstract using either of the terms. If he finds a glass in the room, he knows that a glass might be either empty or full. A wastebasket can be full, and it can be empty. And the same goes for a cardboard box or a bookshelf. He needs to use his imagination as he searches for objects and tries to visualize both opposite characteristics.

HOW TO PLAY: The object of the game, as described above, is to find as many objects as possible that can be described by a given set of opposites. Each player takes a turn choosing two opposing categories: *short/tall, round/square, fast/slow,* and the like. Taking turns, each player finds and names a type of object or person that could fit both categories. For example: *Short/tall.* A waitress could be short or tall; a glass can be short or tall; a plant could be short or tall. The last person to find something to fit the opposing categories is the winner of that round. A new set of opposites is chosen and the game is repeated.

HINTS AND VARIATIONS: This might be more difficult for preschoolers, and parents might want to play in teams with them. You might need to help with the idea of opposites by supplying the first example and letting your child give its opposite. For example, you might say a plant could be tall and allow him to say that a plant could be short. Give praise for choosing unusually and challenging opposite categories—*dull/shiny, smooth/rough*—as that involves as much creative thinking as coming up with the answers.

When in a creative mood, my boys came up with *scrawny/ humongous* to describe the neighborhood cats as well as their owners.

RECALL

PURPOSE: This game helps your child improve her visual memory skills and develops her ability to read for detail.

MATERIALS NEEDED: A book. Try to use books that are a part of your child's homework.

NUMBER OF PLAYERS: 2 to 4.

TIME: Allow at least 30 minutes for this game, since everyone will have to read the same passage.

SKILLS DEVELOPED: The ability to remember the details of what is read is crucial to the understanding of a passage. In order to recall the facts of a paragraph, your child must focus on the details of the written material and fit them together into a complete idea. She can develop her memory with practice and this game encourages that practice by presenting both a challenge and a reward. She will be learning how to concentrate and will improve her attention span.

Most tests—both teacher-made and standardized—require this ability in order to pass. As adults, we are constantly expected to remember the details of what we read, either for our jobs outside of the home (newscaster, stockbroker, letter carrier) or for our "jobs" inside the home (family chef, children's nurse, in-house plumber).

HOW TO PLAY: The object of the game is to remember as many details as possible about a passage read silently from a book. Choose a paragraph in a book that can be read by all the players. Together, the players read the paragraph silently and then the page will be turned over. The players, in turn, will tell one detail they remember about the paragraph. Play continues around the circle until the players run out of details. The last player to remember a detail that has not been previously described will be the winner. Since the first player has an advantage, rotate the first turn for each round.

If all the players cannot read, you can use a picture with a great deal of action. The players will be allowed the same amount of time to look at the picture before it is turned over. Players, in turn, will tell what they remember about the picture. The last player to remember a new detail wins.

HINTS AND VARIATIONS: Use books your child has brought home from school. This is a good way to help her to do her homework and give her an incentive to remember what she has read.

Since you will have an easier time reading the passage and remembering the details, this may present a competition problem. One way to remedy this is for you to read the paragraph aloud to everyone and then the players can tell the details. While this method of play will not improve visual memory skills, it will improve listening skills. If your child has a reading difficulty, and the teacher has suggested that you read her homework with her, this is a good way to help her complete it in a reasonable amount of time.

PASSWORD

PURPOSE: This game exposes your child to rich vocabulary and encourages him to connect words with their meanings.

MATERIALS NEEDED: Children's magazines, schoolbooks, or resource books (such as an encyclopedia or a thesaurus), pencils, and index cards or small pieces of paper.

NUMBER OF PLAYERS: At least 2, better with 3 or more.

TIME: Allow 10 to 15 minutes for each round.

SKILLS DEVELOPED: When a child is stimulated to improve his vocabulary, his interest in reading is also stimulated. When he is more successful in obtaining the meaning from what he reads, he is more eager to take risks in his learning by trying to read more advanced material. In this game he must choose a secret word that the other players are to identify. Because he provides clues to help the other players guess his word, he will need to be aware of synonyms of the words he chooses.

Standardized tests throughout elementary and high school call for a child to understand synonyms and multiple meanings for words. This will also help in doing crossword puzzles, since most clues given are synonyms of the word needed to fill in the puzzle.

HOW TO PLAY: Players in turn choose a word from a magazine, book, dictionary, or other reference source and copy a word, secretly, on a piece of paper. The presenter then gives word clues to all the other players, who try to guess the secret word. For example, for the secret word *cockpit*, the clues might be *plane officer, controls, pilot, place*. The presenting player would say *plane officer* and allow the others to shout out their guesses for the secret word. If no one gets the correct word, the presenter says *control*. Play continues with the presenter giving clues and the others making guesses until the secret word is discovered. If no one can guess the word, the presenter wins that round.

HINTS AND VARIATIONS: Preschool children can play this in teams. They would not be able to write the words, but they could choose words from a picture book for someone else to write down. Allow the child to give clues of more than one word if it is the only way he can do so successfully. You will be aiming for the child to use a synonym, but he might not be ready to function at that level.

This is a game that can be played in a car or restaurant without the benefit of pencil and paper. In this case, everyone will have to trust each other not to change the chosen word midway through the round.

If only two people are playing, set a time. The person to guess the secret word of the other player in the shortest amount of time is the winner.

WHICH SENTENCE?

PURPOSE: This game encourages imaginative thinking and an understanding of how ideas go together to form sentences.

MATERIALS NEEDED: A book (perhaps a schoolbook), pencils, and paper.

NUMBER OF PLAYERS: 4 to 6.

TIME: Allow 15 minutes for each round.

SKILLS DEVELOPED: This game helps your child develop reading and writing skills. When she is the presenter, she must choose a sentence to read from a book and present each word by only its beginning letter. When she is the player, she must formulate complete sentences using words that begin with specific letters. She will develop a better understanding of how reading and writing are related as she sees that the words in the book are just someone else's ideas written down. In the process of playing, some of the mystery and uncertainty will be taken out of both of these skills. She will be able to use her own creativity to try to stump players who might be better readers.

HOW TO PLAY: The object of this game is to create a sentence that other players will choose as the one having come from a book. Each presenter, in turn, chooses any sentence from a book and tells the other players the first letter of each word in that sentence. The other players create sentences using the beginning letters in the order given, write their sentences on a piece of paper, and hand the paper to the presenter. The presenter copies the actual sentence on a piece of paper and then reads all sentences aloud, in random order, to the other players. For example, the sentence chosen from the book for *E*,

C, H, F, W could be *Every car has four wheels.* Created sentences might include: *Each cat has five wives* or *Eating candy helps fifty ways.*

Each player guesses which sentence she thinks is the original by holding her hand up for the one she chooses when they are read the second time. A player receives 1 point for guessing the correct sentence and another for having someone choose her sentence. The player with the most points wins.

HINTS AND VARIATIONS: This game is better with 4 or more players. So bring in the neighbors! Why not invite your child's friends over on a rainy afternoon?

In order to play this game alone with your child, you can take a turn giving the first letters of the words in a chosen sentence. The other player must tell what she thinks the sentence is, based on the context of the book from which the sentence came. A point is awarded for each word that is the same as the one in the original sentence. The player with the most points at the end of the allotted time is the winner.

My students particularly enjoy this game since it gives them a chance to rewrite history. The sentence *Benjamin Franklin was a great American writer* was changed to *Benjamin Franklin wanted a giant African watermelon* and *Benjamin Franklin wore a green angora waistcoat.* Sometimes we just laugh and forget about points.

WRITE
NOW

Helping Your Child
Develop Writing Skills

In our society, a person is judged by his ability to use language effectively, to organize thoughts, and to express himself. As your child's spoken language improves, so does the way people regard him. Think of the child you see in the grocery store who points instead of asking for what he wants. We form an immediate impression—right or wrong—of his intelligence.

Once your child enters school, he will need to apply his language skills in a more advanced way. In addition to speaking clearly, his teachers will expect him to develop an ability to write. Writing requires a more advanced level of language and thought. However, many abilities have to come together before your child can actually begin to write as a means of expression.

Before he can even begin to write, he must be able to hold a pencil or a crayon. It takes a lot of practice with scribbling and making shapes before he can begin to make letters. He also has to understand oral language. A major breakthrough in the writing process comes when he learns that writing is spoken language in written form.

Sometimes children are reluctant to put words on paper because they are not sure of the exact spelling or because they might be given a poor grade as a result of faulty punctuation or a forgotten capital letter. But if we tell our children that we are interested in the content of the writing, not the mechanics, we allow them to shine in terms of creativity and imagination. Spelling, capitalization, and punctuation skills will be introduced and drilled in your child's classroom. When your child writes at home, however, let him be as creative with his spelling as he is with his content. This may be difficult for you at first, but you will find your child will be more expressive when allowed some freedom from traditional rules.

That doesn't mean spelling is not important. In fact, we have included some games that will work on your child's spelling skills. And, of course, you will reinforce your child's spelling when you help him with his homework.

When children are allowed to express themselves freely, there are no right or wrong answers. Through the process of writing, your child not only learns how to write but also has the opportunity to explore ideas and feelings. He becomes more alert to his environment and is better able to remember the things he has written. To be able to produce a piece of written work that is praised for its creativity and content is a tremendous esteem builder. And self-esteem, in turn, is very important to the writing process.

An unwise editor told Louisa May Alcott she would never be able to write anything that would appeal to the general public. It is lucky for us that she did not give up, but determination in the face of such negativity is rare.

We do not want our children to experience this type of negativity. We want them to feel good about their written work and about their creativity. Everyone enjoys doing what they do well. When we help our children succeed, they naturally want to continue the process.

Unfortunately, there is not enough encouragement for this type of activity in our elementary schools. Writing was once an integral part of the elementary school day. It was woven into all the content areas. Some enlightened school systems have made "writing through the curriculum" part of their strategy to improve writing skills, but many school systems now teach writing as a separate course with little relationship to the child's other school activities. These skills cannot be taught in isolation.

So, how can we help our children? The Department of Education study *What Works* states, "Children who are encouraged to draw and scribble 'stories' at an early age will later learn to compose more easily, more effectively, and with greater confidence than children who do not have this encouragement." They found that children became more effective writers when they were encouraged to choose their own topics and to write about them.

One of the most important writing activities you can do with your child is simply to have him write. Young children love to show off what they have done when they feel their work is appreciated. How many of his talents are displayed on your refrigerator right now?

Children get to display their accomplishments with pride when they create their own books. They enjoy making books and they love to read them to their parents, grandparents, neighbors, or anyone else who drops by. And the books can provide a memorable scrapbook for you.

Provide your child with blank pieces of paper, cardboard, file folders, or any materials you have around the house. Encourage him to draw a picture on each page and to write a sentence or two about each picture. Elementary school children love any excuse to draw. The pictures can be sequenced to create a story, or each page can shine independently. As your child's skills develop, encourage him to include more words than pictures. When complete, these books can be enjoyed over and over and will provide a variation for read-aloud time. One of my prized possessions is a book created by my five-year-old about his sneakers. On the first page, he drew a picture of a brand new pair of shoes. *New,* he wrote. The second page showed the same pair of shoes following an adventure in a mud puddle—*dirty.* He illustrated page 3 with the sneakers going into the washing machine—*help,* he wrote. On page 4 the sneakers were as new as on page 1—*new again.* It might have been an advertisement for a laundry detergent! When I read the book again recently, I was warmed to notice it had been dedicated to *Mom and Dad.*

Recently, I discovered a contract written by my son when he was in the third grade. I told him that he would have to convince me that he and his brother could work out a way to share the television cooperatively. He decided to draw up a contract.

In the first section of the contract he wrote, "Whenever a disagreement over T.V. occurs, a coin flip must happen. The coin must either hit the floor or be flipped by an adult to avoid mistrust. I am always heads, no matter what, and my brother is always tales [*sic*]. A flip is for one show. No unneeded name calling!"

By writing the contract he took control over his actions. I no longer had to mediate their disagreements over television watching. That felt great!

The activities in this book recognize that children cannot be hurried through the stages of development, but they can be encouraged to experiment as much as possible within each stage to prepare for the next.

The activities in this section do not focus on the mechanics of writing. There are no punctuation drills or capitalization quizzes. Instead, they emphasize the creative aspects of writing and thinking skills. As your child writes he will reach for the mechanical skills (capitalization, punctuation, complete sentence formation) he needs. You can help him then.

If your child is not developmentally ready to put letters on paper, he can still participate in those activities that require writing by having an adult or older child record his thoughts. The thought organization process will be the same, only the mechanical act of putting the words on the paper will be left for later development. If he can form the letters, have him write the words so he can read them back later.

The skills emphasized in these games include explanation, generalization, prediction, imagination, defending, inferring, and summarizing. These are the skills your child will need to become a creative thinker and a creative writer. So sharpen those pencils and have a great time!

WHAT IS IT?

PURPOSE: This is a game that encourages your child to use language to meet his needs.

MATERIALS NEEDED: No special materials are needed. It can be played any time you are waiting with your child.

NUMBER OF PLAYERS: 2 or the whole family.

TIME: Allow 5 minutes for each round.

SKILLS DEVELOPED: Before your child can learn to write, she must be able to observe, think, and translate her thoughts into words. The skill of observing what is around her makes a child more aware of her environment and its effect on her. She must think about those observations before she can translate her thoughts into clear sentences.

This activity encourages the child to look critically at all items around her. If it is her turn to choose an object, she must try to determine which object might be the most difficult to guess. If she is the guesser, she must try to predict the other players' choices, keenly observe all items around her, and form critical questions that will help her discover the secret object. When she is able to formulate a question, she is using language to get the information she needs to win the game.

HOW TO PLAY: The object of the game is for the opponents to guess a secret object chosen by a given player. Present this game as an activity for spies. You have to be a good "looker" as well as a good listener and you must be able to keep a secret. One player at a time chooses an object in the room, but keeps her choice a secret. Opponents take turns asking yes/no questions to receive clues about the location or the identity of the object. The player who correctly guesses the mystery object wins. Who knows, this game might prepare your child for a career in the secret service.

Example: In a restaurant the item might be the saltshaker. Questions might include: *"Is it on a person?" "Is it on the floor?" "Is it on the wall?" "Do we use it for eating?" "Would I want to take it to school?"*

HINTS AND VARIATIONS: Use discretion in limiting a round if it appears that no one is going to be able to guess the object. In that case, the person who chose the object becomes the winner since she was able to stump the other players. If you are playing with older children, or if you are in a car where everything is going by quickly, you can allow them to uses secret objects that can't be seen. This encourages them to rely more on their imagination and makes everyone more creative in choosing their secret objects.

ADD ONS

PURPOSE: This game provides practice in creating descriptive and unusual sentences.

MATERIALS NEEDED: Paper and pencils.

NUMBER OF PLAYERS: This game is fun with 3 or 4 players, but 2 people can still have a good time.

TIME: Allow 15 to 30 minutes.

SKILLS DEVELOPED: The game encourages your child to extend a given sentence by using information he has learned from different sources. He will need to follow a logical sequence while experimenting with words and adding on to sentences. He will also need to visualize situations in his mind in order to describe these situations. This is a skill that is difficult for most children because television has begun to do the visualizing for them, leaving little to their imagination. As a result, children are losing the ability to create their own pictures in their heads.

HOW TO PLAY: In this game, the object is to add words to a given sentence to make a new sentence. Taking turns, each player says a two-word sentence, which contains a noun and a verb. For example, *Girls eat.*

Each player, including the presenting player, writes a sentence using those two words and as many other words as possible to create a more elaborate sentence. Players could add words which tell how many, how large, what shape, what color, when, where, how, what, and so on. The sentence might become, *Two skinny girls eat round, yellow popsicles at the county fair.* Each player receives a point for each word that is added appropriately to the sentence and the player with the most points wins.

HINTS AND VARIATIONS: For younger players, and in situations where you are without pencil and paper, each player, in turn, adds a word or words to the sentence to create a new sentence without writing anything down. Play continues until no one is able to add new words. The winner is the player who adds the last word. The sentences given at each turn must be complete. For example, the first turn would be, *Two girls eat.* The next, *Two girls eat popsicles.* Then, *Two skinny girls eat popsicles,* and so on. Be careful not to overuse any particular type of word. If you allow too many color words, for example, the sentence could go on forever. I learned this the hard way. In one of my classes, a student took the sentence *Many balloons flew* and created *Many yellow, blue, purple, black, red, brown, pink balloons flew* before I invoked a two-color rule.

SOUNDS LIKE

PURPOSE: This game provides practice in categorizing words by beginning sounds.

MATERIALS NEEDED: Papers, pencils, and a timer.

NUMBER OF PLAYERS: Any number can play.

TIME: Allow 15 to 30 minutes for several rounds.

SKILLS DEVELOPED: This game motivates your child to think of words she knows and to analyze them to determine if they fit into a particular sound pattern. She will develop her attentiveness to words and will be able to break them into beginning and ending sounds.

HOW TO PLAY: The object here is to list as many words as possible that begin with a particular sound. Each player takes a turn presenting a letter sound, or a short blend (*sh, st, ch*), to the other players. All players, including the presenter, write as many words as they can think of in 3 minutes that begin with that sound. For example, if the letter sound chosen is hard *c*, players could list *cat, car,* or *kitten*. If the letter chosen is *s*, players could list *sea, soup,* or *celery*. At the end of the time, each player reads her list and all words that appear on more than one list are eliminated. Points are given for any word that is not on any other list, and the player with the most points wins.

HINTS AND VARIATIONS: Spelling does not count here as long as your child can read the word herself. Accept any approximation. Adjust the writing time to the ages of the players. Younger children might need longer than 3 minutes and older children may need less time. You will be able to tell how much time is needed after you play one or two times.

For younger children, you can be the recorder, or younger and older children can play in teams. Here is another place you could use your child's vocabulary words as a starting point for the activity. You could also change the activity so that the words written have to have the same ending, rather than beginning, sound as the clue word. They would not have to rhyme, but merely end with the same letter—*word, hard, forward, fried.*

PLEASE PUT WORDS IN MY MOUTH

PURPOSE: In this game, your child practices creating sentences.

MATERIALS NEEDED: Comic strips without words, or with words cut off or whited out, pencils, and paper.

NUMBER OF PLAYERS: 3 or more.

TIME: Allow 10 to 20 minutes.

SKILLS DEVELOPED: Your child's attention span and interpretation skills will become more developed with this game. It provides practice in creating complete sentences as part of a story. "Please Put Words in My Mouth" will help your child analyze situations and become more aware of cause and effect.

The skills developed with this game will help your child better understand the charts, graphs, and pictures often featured in textbooks. This game reinforces the values of sportsmanship and fair play, since the winner is determined by a vote of the other players. It also requires a sense of humor.

HOW TO PLAY: The object of the game is to create complete sentences to describe or accompany a picture. Begin with comic strips from the newspaper or from a comic book. Use one frame of the strip for each round of the game. All players are shown the same frame and they must write a complete sentence of dialogue appropriate to the picture. When all the sentences are written, the players read them aloud and vote on which sentence is the best in describing the situation creatively.

HINTS AND VARIATIONS: With younger children, you can play in teams, or you and an older child could help a younger one in creating his sentences. This is a good game for the child who has difficulty with reading and writing skills because creativity is the most important component of the game.

Your child's dialogue might describe the situation or it may offer a funny explanation for what is happening in the strip. The more creative the dialogue, the more fun it is to play.

For example, when playing with my son, we used a frame showing a snowball chasing Garfield down the hill. My sentence *Garfield is running down the hill being chased by a giant snowball* was accurate, but my son's sentence *A snowball from space raced Garfield to the house for dinner* was much funnier.

Save comic strips for several days so that you will have many choices to use for the game. If you are playing with two players, each player can choose his own comic strip and write as many sentences as possible to create a short paragraph suggesting what the character is saying. This becomes more of a shared experience than a competitive game and is a fun way for you to help your child develop his writing skills. You might even enjoy creating dialogue together for the same comic strip.

LICENSE TO PLAY

PURPOSE: This game encourages your child to use complete sentences and provides practice in sentence building.

MATERIALS NEEDED: No special materials, but players must be in view of car license plates.

NUMBER OF PLAYERS: 2 or a car full.

TIME: Allow 5 minutes or less for each round.

SKILLS DEVELOPED: The ability to respond in complete sentences is the way we inform others of what we know and understand. In school, a child must write spelling words and answer test and discussion questions in complete sentences. In most cases, she will have some information (the spelling word or the clues of the question), but she will have to generate the rest of the sentence herself.

This activity encourages your child to complete sentences relying mainly on her inner resources with very few guidelines. She will have to use nouns and verbs even if she doesn't yet know what they are.

The way we communicate is the first thing people notice about us, and often judgments are made about us based on that first impression. We've all met the person who answers "Huh?" to every question and have wondered about her intellectual ability. The ability to generate sentences in order to express ourselves enables us to make ourselves understood. When your child sees that she can have her needs met through language, it gives her the confidence she'll need to venture out into the world.

HOW TO PLAY: The object of the game is to be the first player to create a complete sentence using the letters on a car license plate as the first letter of each of the words in the sentence. One player notices a license plate that contains two or more letters and announces the letters to the other players. All players, as soon as possible, call out complete sentences made up of words that begin with the letters as they appear on the license plate. For example: *BPA—Boys pick apples.* The first player to arrive at a complete sentence can choose the next plate.

HINTS AND VARIATIONS: Give yourself a handicap by trying to make your sentence more complex than those your child might create. This will allow your child a chance to win and will prove an example of the type of sentence you hope she will eventually begin to create. By using descriptive words in your sentences, you show how to use words to make sentences more colorful. For example: *Boys play appropriately.* You might want to exempt the driver from choosing the license plate since she should be spending her time looking at the road!

SENTENCE FUN

PURPOSE: This game provides practice in creating sentences using specific, often unrelated words.

MATERIALS NEEDED: Pencils and paper.

NUMBER OF PLAYERS: 3 or more (see Hints and Variations for possibilities with 2 players).

TIME: Allow 15 to 30 minutes.

SKILLS DEVELOPED: Your child will explore the possible ways of combining words, resulting in the imaginative use of language. He will develop a better understanding of how words go together to create a complete sentence. This game provides an opportunity for you to teach your child to respect the rights and feelings of others. "Sentence Fun" encourages sportsmanship and fair play. The winner is determined by vote and it is important for all players to realize that everyone is a winner if he is having a good time.

HOW TO PLAY: The object of the game is to create a complete sentence using predetermined words. Each player, in turn, names three words that everyone must use in creating a sentence. These words do not have to relate to one another. In fact, the game is most challenging and fun when they do not relate. Everyone, including the presenting player, creates a sentence using those three words and as many other words as he wants to make a creative sentence.

For example, the three words might be *rain, leaf, bottle*. A sentence using these words could be as simple as, *I watched the rain fall on a leaf and a bottle*, or as complex as *While I was walking in the rain, I slipped on a leaf and fell on a bottle*. Each player reads his sentence aloud and everyone votes on the most creative sentence that makes sense. The player whose sentence is chosen is the winner.

HINTS AND VARIATIONS: When playing with younger children, have them say the sentence aloud without having to write it down. This will also increase the competition because the other players will hear what the previous player has said and will be challenged to come up with a better sentence. You could also play in teams and you could do the writing for the younger child. The words can be chosen from school words, kitchen words, restaurant words, or words appropriate to any setting where the game is played. This game worked well while I was making dinner and both boys wanted my attention.

Without paper and pencil, it becomes a great waiting game. If playing with only 2 players, each player can present three words for the other player to use in making a sentence. Since there are only two of you, you can eliminate the vote. Everyone wins this way.

If you want to add the element of chance, play with a game board. Each player, in turn, presents three words to the next player, who must make a sentence using those words. The player who makes the sentence then rolls the dice and moves around the game board. If your child cannot come up with a sentence, gently suggest one to him and see if he can come up with a variation of yours.

BLANKETY BLANKS

PURPOSE: This game provides practice in developing sentences with creativity and imagination.

MATERIALS NEEDED: Paper and pencils.

NUMBER OF PLAYERS: Best with more than 2 players, but 2 can get something out of it, too.

TIME: Allow 10 to 20 minutes.

SKILLS DEVELOPED: This game provides opportunities for sentence development and allows your child to explore and play with words and word combinations with a strategy in mind. She will write a sentence, and then eliminate one of the words. She will need to think of possible words that can be used in her created sentence and she must anticipate which words other players might use.

HOW TO PLAY: The objective is to place a word in a sentence that is the same word eliminated by the presenting player. Each player, in turn, writes a sentence she has created, leaving out one word that is important to the sentence. For example, the sentence might be, *Joe was so tired he put his _____ on the table.* Each player, including the player who created the sentence, writes one word that could go in the blank space on a separate piece of paper. The players read their chosen words aloud, and each player who matches the word of the presenting player receives a point. The game continues with a new presenter and a new sentence. The player with the most points wins. If no one matches the presenter, the latter gets a point.

HINTS AND VARIATIONS: This game can be played without writing the sentence. The creation of the sentence with the missing element is more important than the actual writing. You don't want to make your child uncomfortable if she is not able to write or spell correctly, and it is often easier for a young child to create a sentence orally than to write it down. She should write the one word to fill in the blank, however.

A variation of this game for only 2 players would be for each player to write as many words as possible to fill in the blank. Identical responses are eliminated and players get 1 point for each unique and logical response. Another variation for 2 or more players is for each player, in turn, to say a word that could fill in the blank. The last player to be able to suggest an appropriate word is the winner. This will allow your child to use her powers of persuasion to convince you that her word makes sense.

RAP IT UP

PURPOSE: Here's another game that encourages practice in making sentences while allowing your child to be creative and imaginative.

MATERIALS NEEDED: Papers and pencils.

NUMBER OF PLAYERS: Any number can play.

TIME: Allow 15 to 30 minutes.

SKILLS DEVELOPED: This game helps reinforce the rhyming skills that are so important in teaching reading readiness in kindergarten and first grade. It also helps develop sentence-building skills. Your child can be creative and imaginative in his sentence building while he searches for rhyming patterns.

HOW TO PLAY: The object of the game is to create sentences that rhyme. Players take turns starting the rhyme. The first player writes a sentence that is the first line of a poem. Each player, in turn, adds a line that follows the idea of the first sentence. The final word must rhyme with the end of the previous sentence. For example, if the first line is *I see a bear,* the next line might be *He had no hair.* The players continue adding additional lines until a player is unable to add any more. The last player to add a line gets a point. The player with the most points is the winner. If it is not possible to add a second line to the poem, the player who started the poem receives a point.

The rhyming style is one young people are very familiar with since they hear rap singers rhyme each day on the radio.

HINTS AND VARIATIONS: With younger children, you can play this game without actually writing anything down. Each player would say his line instead of writing it. The goal is to create a sentence with a final word that rhymes. Remember, writing is simply talk written down. This is a good way to come up with a personalized message to send as a birthday or get-well card, and your child could add a picture to go along with the poem. My boys hated to write thank-you notes, and this was one way we could do it together and have fun.

In order to start the creative juices flowing, you could even start with the picture drawing and have the poem relate to the picture. You could also encourage your child to use one of his spelling words in each line of the poem. It might also be fun to read some rhymes during your read-aloud time as an introduction to this game.

COMP AND CON

PURPOSE: This game encourages vocabulary development and fosters an understanding of how things are alike and different.

MATERIALS NEEDED: Paper and pencils.

NUMBER OF PLAYERS: 2 to 6.

TIME: Allow 15 to 30 minutes.

SKILLS DEVELOPED: "Comp and Con" encourages your child to come up with descriptive words that fit a pair of objects such as *tree/ship, television/VCR*. This will help develop a better understanding of the meanings of words and how they relate to other words. She will see that the things around us have many different features.

HOW TO PLAY: In this game, players list words or complete sentences that describe two objects. Each player, in turn, names two objects. All players then make a list on a piece of paper of all the ways in which the two objects are alike and how they are different. For example, for the objects *tree* and *ship*: They are alike in that both float, are wooden, and can be tall. They are different in that trees do not carry people, trees are alive, ships don't grow. When all lists are finished, the players read their answers. Answers that are the same on more than one list are eliminated, and players receive 1 point for each idea that does not appear on another list. If there is a dispute about any of the similarities or differences, the player must defend her choice to the satisfaction of the other players. If your child can argue that a ship and a tree are alike because they both make people happy, let her use her persuasive language skills to justify the comparison.

HINTS AND VARIATIONS: This game can also be played without pencil and paper with younger children or while you are waiting for a meal or an appointment. With this variation, each player, in turn, names one way in which the objects are alike and one way in which they are different. The last player to be able to compare and contrast the objects is the winner. The power of persuasion is also very useful when played this way.

WHERE'S IT BELONG?

PURPOSE: This is another game that provides practice in categorization skills.

MATERIALS NEEDED: Pencils and paper.

NUMBER OF PLAYERS: 2 to 4.

TIME: Allow 15 to 20 minutes.

SKILLS DEVELOPED: This game helps your child to expand his vocabulary and to make generalizations about words and ideas. "Where's It Belong?" encourages him to be more alert to his environment in order to build up ideas for future sessions of the game. While playing, he will be developing a new way of noticing things in his world because he will begin to relate each thing he sees to a category, for instance, people, blue things, things made of glass. He may have to defend his choice of a particular item as part of a category and this will improve his thinking skills.

HOW TO PLAY: The object of the game is to create a list of words that belong in a particular category and do not appear on the other players' lists. Each player takes a turn naming a category—*dogs, large things, weather*. All players, including the presenting player, write as many items as they can that belong to that category. For example, for the *dogs* category, a list might include *huskies, terriers, mutts, goldens*. When the lists are complete, each player reads his list. Those items that appear on more than one list are eliminated. Players receive 1 point for each word that is not on any other list. If a player includes an item in a category that the other players feel does not belong, the player must defend his choice to the satisfaction of the other players. "Where's It Belong?" is similar to "Picka" in the reading section and provides another example that writing is simply talk written down.

HINTS AND VARIATIONS: Do not make correct spelling a part of this game. Allow your child to be just as creative in his spelling as in his choice of words. My sons could come up with many examples they couldn't spell. If they had worried about spelling, I would have missed out on a *wrecked car* in the *flat* category or *gorilla* in the *strong* category. Be open to unusual responses. If your child can defend *Darryl Strawberry* as an example of *fruit*, give credit for it. You want to encourage imagination.

If playing with younger children, play in teams so they will not be excluded by the inability to write. Feel free to offer suggestions of possible categories, but be sure to offer more than one idea so the presenting player can choose the one he wants to use. Your child must feel that he has some control over the direction of the game in order to feel a part of it.

DESCRIPTIONS

PURPOSE: This game motivates your child to use language creatively.

MATERIALS NEEDED: Pictures, pencils, paper, and a timer. Use magazine or newspaper pictures or family photos.

NUMBER OF PLAYERS: 2 or more.

TIME: Allow 15 to 20 minutes.

SKILLS DEVELOPED: This game encourages your child to be more attentive to her environment and to develop a facility with words that describe what she sees. She must grasp the meaning of pictures that have no words and translate that understanding to language. She will also be listening to words you use and will thus develop her vocabulary. When lists of words are compared, players might have to defend their choices, and they will need to use language effectively to prove their point.

HOW TO PLAY: The object of the game is to use words that are not used by any other players to describe a picture. Limit responses to individual descriptive words, since it is very difficult to compare phrases objectively. Choose a picture from a magazine or family album. Each player may look at it for one minute. Each player then makes a list of words that describe the picture. When all lists are complete, the words on the lists are read off and all the words that appear on more than one list are eliminated. If words appear on a list that do not seem to apply to the picture, give the player an opportunity to explain why she chose that word. For example, in a picture of children jumping rope, describing words might be *happy, playful, joyful, smiling*. A child using the word *hot* could argue that the children would not be wearing shorts if it were not hot outside. Each player receives a point for the words on her list that were not on any other list. The player with the most points wins.

HINTS AND VARIATIONS: If playing with younger children, each player could say a word aloud that describes the picture. The last to name a describing word is the winner. You or an older child might want to write down the words by all players to guard against duplication. This would be a good time to use pictures in schoolbooks to help your child review her homework.

Be careful if choosing a picture of yourself. I was surprised by some of the describing words my boys used!

PATTERNS

PURPOSE: This game provides practice in creating sentences that follow a prescribed pattern.

MATERIALS NEEDED: Game board, die, papers, and pencils.

NUMBER OF PLAYERS: 2 to 4.

TIME: Allow 30 minutes.

SKILLS DEVELOPED: "Patterns" encourages your child to follow a logical, sequential order while experimenting with word combinations. He will develop his originality and creativity and find ways to express his ideas. Because he will be creating sentences based on a specific sequence, which is presented by another player, the order imposed by this game will increase his attention to detail.

HOW TO PLAY: The object of the game is to create sentences using a specific series of letters for the beginning letter of each word in the sentence. Each player, in turn, writes a series of letters and shows it to the next player. The series can be in alphabetical order—*A, B, C, D*—or the letters of his name—*E, R, I, C*—or any letters the player wants to use. The number of letters is determined by the players at the beginning of the game.

The next player must create a sentence using the letters provided. For example, *A boy can drive* (A,B,C,D) or *Eagles ride in clouds* (E,R,I,C). If he forms a sentence correctly, he rolls the die and moves around the game board. The play continues. The player who rolls the die then presents his series of letters so the next player can create a sentence. Play continues until someone completes his way around the board.

Using the game board adds an element of chance to the game and provides the younger player with an equal opportunity to win.

HINTS AND VARIATIONS: Tailor the length of the sentences to the age of your child. For younger children, use a three-letter series. Older children may want to use five or six letters. In the case of children who cannot yet write, allow them to create their sentences orally, or you can play in teams with you writing the sentence your child creates.

CREATIVE CRITIQUERS

PURPOSE: This game motivates your child to use her sentence-making skills as she watches television in a more creative way.

MATERIALS NEEDED: Surprise, this game is played in front of the television! You will also need paper and pencils.

NUMBER OF PLAYERS: Minimum of 2, but the more the merrier (excellent game for the entire family).

TIME: Allow 15 to 20 minutes in addition to the time spent watching the television program.

SKILLS DEVELOPED: This game provides practice with critical thinking, analyzing, and summarizing. It develops the ability to look at a whole situation and to break it down into its parts. Your child will have to be attentive to details and alert to how those details relate to each other and to the entire program. It should produce a more critical television viewer and make your child more selective. This game could inspire your child to one day become a screenwriter or film critic.

HOW TO PLAY: The object of the game is to create a review of a television program with as many details and as much analysis as possible. Players must agree to watch the same program. Each player can decide for herself whether she will keep the pencil and paper out during the show and take notes, or whether she will rely on her memory of the total program. (If you are playing with your child, encourage her to keep notes while you rely on memory.) At the end of the program, each player writes a summary of the program using as many details as possible. She makes judgments, both positive and negative, about the parts of the show that were meaningful to her. For example, after watching the "Cosby Show," the summary may include a description of the people and their home as well as whether the situation was one that might happen in your home. Your child might compare how a situation was handled on the television program with how it might have been handled in your home. Critiques are compared. Scoring here is objective. If you feel it is necessary to declare a winner, base your decision on the total number of details.

HINTS AND VARIATIONS: Younger children can be allowed to give their summaries orally after you have written yours. Another variation would allow each player to earn points for each object she noticed that no one else saw. This variation is easier for younger children because they would be able to list objects they noticed rather than events. Each player would read her list and duplicate items would be eliminated. You could even encourage debate over a particular point. In order to play without any writing at all, each player could state an object or event, in turn, and the last player to remember a detail would be declared the winner.

My boys also found it fun to analyze commercials. Since they are shorter than an entire program, the activity can be done quickly if time is an issue.

NAME IT

PURPOSE: This game helps your child develop vocabulary as well as the powers of observation.

MATERIALS NEEDED: Paper and pencils.

NUMBER OF PLAYERS: 2 to 4.

TIME: Allow 15 to 30 minutes.

SKILLS DEVELOPED: This game encourages your child to recognize how words can express character traits and how those traits can apply to a particular individual. For example, the word *moody* might make us think of someone we know who is happy one minute and grumpy the next. The need to find the perfect words to describe a person or situation is a skill he will use throughout school while searching for the best word to use in a report or a project. Your child will develop his visual attention skills as he concentrates on an individual's particular characteristics and then labels the characteristics on his list. He might one day use this talent if he becomes a psychologist, a portrait painter, a poet, or a private detective.

HOW TO PLAY: The object of the game is to use unique words to describe another player. Each player's name, in turn, is used for the activity. Both the first and last names are written down the left-hand side of a piece of paper.

M	Music lover
I	Ice cream eater
C	Chummy
H	Hairy
A	Amiable
E	Exciting
L	Lively
R	Rowdy
O	Ornery
S	Sincere
S	Smiling

All players, on their own, write words or phrases beginning with each of the letters that describe the person whose name is being used. At the end of the allotted time, each player reads the words or phrases he has written. All entries that are on more than one list are eliminated. Players receive 1 point for each word or phrase that was not used by any of the other players. The player with the most points wins.

HINTS AND VARIATIONS: If, after playing this game often, you have used the names of the entire family and circle of friends, use the name of a person in the neighborhood, in the news, or on television. With older children you might also describe objects. This is much more abstract and difficult. For example, in describing a chair, you might say, _close to the floor, hard, at the table, in the living room, restful._ Since you do not count spelling, each child should read his own list.

HEADS UP

PURPOSE: "Heads Up" provides practice with spelling and with vocabulary development.

MATERIALS NEEDED: Paper, pencils, and a dictionary.

NUMBER OF PLAYERS: 2 to 4.

TIME: Allow 15 to 30 minutes.

SKILLS DEVELOPED: Most children can use practice in reinforcing spelling and vocabulary. With this game, your child will have to call to mind or look up words that fit a particular spelling pattern.

Looking up words exposes her to new vocabulary and placing words on the chart makes her more aware of spelling patterns.

HOW TO PLAY: The object of the game is to fill in words on a chart that are different from the words used by other players. One player chooses a four-, five-, or six-letter guide word. All players write the guide word vertically in both the left-hand and the right-hand margin of their sheet of paper. In the left-hand margin, the word is spelled from top to bottom; and in the right-hand margin, it is written from bottom to top. Each player then writes words that fit into the chart created by the letters. For example, if the word *stop* is the one written up and down the margins, the first word filled in must begin with *S* and end with *P*. The second word must begin with *T* and end with *O,* and so on.

S	tam	P
T	emp	O
O	bjec	T
P	as	S

Players may use words they know, or they may use a dictionary to find words to fit the pattern. When using a dictionary, they must be able to pronounce the words they choose. When all lists are complete, players compare lists. Words that are on more than one list are eliminated. Players receive 1 point for any word remaining on the list. The player with the most points wins.

HINTS AND VARIATIONS: Use this game to help your child study for spelling by using spelling words as the guide words. Try to keep your words at a level close to your child's so that she will have an opportunity to win. You can do this by limiting your words to those found in a child's dictionary or by using ones that are the length she might use.

REBUS

PURPOSE: This game gives your child practice in creating complete sentences while translating the spoken word into pictures.

MATERIALS NEEDED: Pencils or crayons, and paper.

NUMBER OF PLAYERS: 3 to 6.

TIME: Allow 15 to 30 minutes.

SKILLS DEVELOPED: This game motivates your child to create a complete sentence in his head and to imagine what it would look like represented by drawings. When your child conveys an idea using drawings rather than words, he gains some insight into ways to present material in nonverbal forms, such as charts or illustrations. This activity helps develop the ability to break down information into its parts and then successfully put the pieces together in an innovative way. For example, the word *canteen* might be represented by a drawing of a can and a teenager together.

HOW TO PLAY: The object of the game is to create a sentence with drawings or individual numbers or letters replacing each of the words. Each player, in turn, creates a sentence and writes the sentence by using pictures, numbers, or letters instead of using the words themselves. For example, *I can see you* would look like this, 👁 🥫 C U . The other players try to read the sentence correctly by shouting out what they think the sentence says. The first player to guess the actual sentence is the winner and has the opportunity to create the next clue sentence. If no one is able to read the sentence, the person who presented it is the winner and gets another chance to present.

HINTS AND VARIATIONS: For younger players, make a chart of the possible rebus (picture) clues and keep it within everyone's sight. Use any combination of picture clues that the players can agree upon. Make sure you allow many actions words (verbs) so that you will have enough to choose from.

For example, run could be 🏃. Be sure the drawings are as simple as possible so the less artistic child won't be intimidated.

This is a great way to improve visual memory because the player who remembers the fastest what the picture clues represent will usually be the one to solve the sentence first.

Since my artistic skills are not my strong point, my boys and I could often laugh at my picture clues. It was a good way for the boys to see that in some areas at least, children have stronger skills than their parents.

ASK ME A QUESTION

PURPOSE: This game helps your child develop the skill of question formation.

MATERIALS NEEDED: Paper and pencils.

NUMBER OF PLAYERS: 2 to 6.

TIME: Allow 15 to 30 minutes.

SKILLS DEVELOPED: Your child uses the skills of visualization and imagination to create a story based on a given math problem. As this game is the reverse of a mathematical word problem, it will help with writing as well as math skills. In a math word problem, your child reads a question about a situation and adds, subtracts, multiplies, or divides the numbers in it to arrive at an answer. In "Ask Me a Question," she begins with the math problem and its answer and creates a question that represents those math facts. She must use words to express math concepts. She will begin to see more clearly how math and language are related and how understanding the language of math can help take some of the mystery out of the subject. This game is difficult to lose, fun to play, and encourages humorous responses.

HOW TO PLAY: The object of the game is to create word problems. Each child, in turn, creates, writes, and then presents a math word problem. The problem presented could be *2 + 2 = 4.* The next player makes up a story that uses that problem and asks a question about the story. For example, the story and question could be: *There are two children playing this game. Two more children come over to play. How many children would be playing?* For each successful story, give 1 point. If the story is incorrect or the player could not create a story, the player who presented the problem receives a point. The player with the most points at the end of the allotted time wins.

HINTS AND VARIATIONS: For play with younger children, or at a time when pencil and paper are not available, allow the players to present the problem orally. This is a good game to play while waiting at a restaurant or for a doctor's appointment. You can even use it to an advantage when tempers are short and everyone is impatient.

Use your child's math homework to find problems on which to base your stories. This is a good way to help her remember her math facts. Don't use problems that are too hard for your child. You are not trying to teach her to multiply. You are trying to help her learn to form questions while reinforcing the skills she is learning at school.

When encouraged to use their hobbies and interests as material for their stories, my boys often came up with more complicated stories than I would have imagined possible. Even simple math facts were interpreted creatively. Here is what my young son's response was when given the problem *1 + 1 + 2 = 4: During last week's baseball game, Andy ended his batting slump. At first it seemed Andy would be sitting on the bench for the next game. His first time at bat, he struck out— again! He was really down, but tried to remind himself that he was up against Chris, one of the Yachtsmen's best pitchers. As lead-off batter in the third inning, he got a single. That was a relief! The next player walked. "Good eye!" his teammates yelled. That brought Travis to bat. He was the team's strongest hitter. He smacked the ball—a strong line drive to the outfield, and Andy slid into homeplate. How many bases did Andy touch during the third inning?*

MAGIC WORD

PURPOSE: "Magic Word" provides practice in spelling and vocabulary development.

MATERIALS NEEDED: Paper, pencils, and a dictionary (optional).

NUMBER OF PLAYERS: 2 to 4.

TIME: Allow at least 15 minutes.

SKILLS DEVELOPED: This game will help your child develop a better understanding of spelling rules. He will see similarities in spelling patterns as he creates new words from old ones, for example: *fat, hat,* or *sat* from *cat.* He will develop his ability to break down words into their letters and letter combinations. He will also need to visualize possible changes by manipulating the letter combinations in his mind.

HOW TO PLAY: The object of the game is for each player to create a new word by changing a letter in a given word. One player chooses the original guide word to be used. This word is written on a piece of paper and shown to the other player. Each player, in turn, may change one letter in the word in order to create a new word. For example, if the guide word is *line,* it can be changed to <u>m</u>ine by the second player, then mi<u>l</u>e by the third player, then <u>t</u>ile by the fourth player, and so on. Each time the word is changed, the new one must be a real word and must be spelled correctly. The winner is the last player able to create a new word.

HINTS AND VARIATIONS: This is a good way to work with spelling assignments and specific vocabulary from schoolbooks. Use the words from school as the given word to allow your child to play with his spelling or vocabulary homework.

Tailor the length of the word to the age of the child. Beginning readers could handle a three-letter word, such as *big.* For example, <u>b</u>ig, <u>p</u>ig, pi<u>t</u>, p<u>o</u>t. Older children can work with four- or five-letter words. Include the nonreading child on a team with you to make him feel part of the game. This is also a way that you can justify instructing as you go.

It is possible to play without paper and pencils if you limit your words to three letters. It might also be a good idea for you to pick the guide word, because you want to be sure that it is a word with many options. Good words to begin with are those with a silent *E* at the end, those with *AI* in the middle, and those ending with *IG, AN,* or *AR.* Let your child use a children's dictionary to help him come up with new words, and he will develop research skills at the same time.

WORDY

PURPOSE: This game gives your child practice in comparing words based on similarities in spelling.

MATERIALS NEEDED: Paper and pencils.

NUMBER OF PLAYERS: 2 to 4.

TIME: Allow 20 to 30 minutes.

SKILLS DEVELOPED: In this game, your child is encouraged to think of words based on the letters they contain and the way the letters are combined. She will develop skills in categorizing words based on length and spelling rules. She will be improving her ability to spell without the drill of studying spelling words as she sees how words often follow common patterns. The game also develops strong concentration skills.

HOW TO PLAY: The object of the game is to discover your opponent's secret word. One player writes a word on a piece of paper and conceals it from the other players. The only clue given about the secret word is the number of letters it contains. The other players, in turn, guess words that have the same number of letters. The presenter lets them know if any of the letters in the guessed word are the same as those in the secret word, but only tells how many. Sounds complicated, but it's very simple. It goes like this.

The presenting player chooses a secret word (for example, *time*). She tells the other players that her secret word has four letters. Each player makes four blanks at the top of her paper. The first player might guess *milk*. All players list the letters *M, I, L, K* under their blanks.

__	__	__	__
M	I	L	K

The presenter tells the first player that the secret word and *milk* have two letters in common. She does not tell her which letters. The next player tries to think of a word that has at least two of the letters found in *milk*. She might guess *lock,* and the players would write that word beneath *milk*.

				Number of correct letters
__	__	__	__	
M	I	L	K	2
L	O	C	K	0

When the presenting player says none of the letters in *lock* are contained in the secret word, the players know that the *L* and *K* in *milk* are not in the secret word either and that *M* and *I* must be two of the letters found in the secret word. This is worked out on their papers by crossing out the letters *definitely not* in the secret word and by placing the letters *definitely in* the secret word on the blanks at the top, one letter per blank.

M	I			Number of correct letters
__	__	__	__	
M	I	L	K	2
L	O	C	K	0

Now the players know two of the letters, but they still don't know where the letters fall in the secret word. The next player would choose a word that contains both *M* and *I*—for example, *dime*. The presenting player would announce that *dime* contains three of the letters in the secret word. Again, players do not know if the secret word contains the *e* or the *d*. So the next player would guess a word containing either an *e* or a *d*, the *i* and *m*, and one of the letters definitely out—*lime*. The players know the *e* is contained in the secret word, because *I* has already been eliminated. The worksheet is then updated.

M	I	E		Number of correct letters
___	___	___	___	
M	I	L	K	2
L	O	C	K	0
D	I	M	E	3
L	I	M	E	3

Now the players know three of the four letters, but they still do not know the order of the letters. The next player guesses a word containing the three known letters and one additional new letter. She might guess *mine* or *mike* or the correct word, *time*. If she does not guess the correct word, the next player gets a chance. If the player guesses a word with four correct letters—*mite*—the presenting player tells her the letters are correct, but in the wrong order. The guesser gets one more chance to guess. The player to guess the secret word is the winner.

Whew! It usually takes one round of this game to become comfortable with the format, but it is well worth the effort.

HINTS AND VARIATIONS: With only 2 players, each player chooses a word for the other player to discover. Keep track of how many guesses it takes each player to figure out the secret word. The player who guesses in the fewest number of turns wins. Be sure to keep the length and difficulty of the words appropriate to the age of the child. You can get a good idea of words to use from their schoolbooks. You would also make this a creative way to get them to do their spelling homework. Use their spelling words, or words with the same spelling pattern, as your secret word. For example, if the spelling list contains words with *or* in them such as *corn*, also use other words with *or*—*torn*, or *fork*.

To make this game easier for younger children, allow the presenting player to tell which letters of the guessed word are in the secret word. For example, if the secret word is *time*, and *milk* is the guess, the presenter would disclose that *m* and *i* are in the secret word.

THREE

COUNT
ME IN

Helping Your Child
Develop Math Skills

I f Matthew took the train from Boston to Baltimore at 7:30 A.M., and the train traveled at 50 miles per hour, but stopped in New York for a 30-minute layover, and Danielle's train traveled from Columbus, Georgia, to Baltimore leaving at 9 A.M., traveling directly at 75 miles per hour, and the distance from Boston to Baltimore is one-third more than the distance from Columbus to New York, how old is Matthew's cat?

For many adults, word problems make no more sense than that. They have struggled with numbers since they were children. Frightened they will pass their fears along, they are uncomfortable trying to help their own children with math skills. Perhaps you are one of those adults. If so, fear not. Even if you are math phobic, you can help your child develop the thinking skills that are fundamental to success in mathematics, and you may even learn to enjoy math in the process.

For some, math comes easily. If you are comfortable with math and want to share your love of numbers and logical thought with your children, dive right in. This section is for you, too.

Children are not born with a fear of math. They love to investigate and to discover, and the process of discovery is uniquely satisfying. It is a real esteem-booster for young children to tackle a challenge and solve it creatively.

A young child responds to math experiences based on what she sees around her. A child in the elementary grades can usually interpret information she sees and can arrive at a simple, logical conclusion. For example, if a kindergarten child knows that there are three snacks and four children in her group, she understands someone is going to have to share.

In the early elementary years, your child will learn the rote math skills of addition, subtraction, multiplication, and division. However, often a child can do a full page of problems that requires one of these four processes, but when expected to determine which process to use in a word problem she doesn't know where to begin. Math has a special language that tells us what to do with numbers. In order to decide which process to use and how to apply it, your child must understand that language. She needs to know that when a problem asks *how many are left,* she should subtract. When a problem asks *how many all together,* she should add.

Math provides children with a method and a language for organizing information. We use math for comparing, ordering, predicting, and graphing. The goal of mathematical learning is to develop problem-solving abilities.

Issues surrounding a child's weekly allowance often present problem-solving opportunities. When my older son's favorite ball was thrown into the ocean by the neighborhood bully, he needed to know how many weeks he would need to save his allowance before he could buy a new one.

Children acquire problem-solving skills at different rates, and the inability to perform as well as other children in the classroom can affect a child's self-esteem. Teachers often recite math problems orally, and each child is given a turn to answer aloud. Some children cannot solve the problem at all. Others do not solve the problem the way the teacher intended. Even though they arrive at the correct answer, their strategy may not satisfy the skill being taught, or the teacher. Children are aware of their inabilities and it becomes quickly obvious which children are the mathematical thinkers and which are not.

You want your child to see herself as a mathematical problem solver whether she is the quickest with the answer in class or not, and whether or not her method of arriving at the solution to a problem is the traditional one. Math phobics are made, not born. Math anxiety comes when a child is made to feel uncomfortable with numbers, and you want to make sure this doesn't happen to your child.

It took a while for my younger child to build his confidence in math. He was often the first to be eliminated during his classroom "math bees." Even though he got As on the math tests that were not timed, he felt dumb in math. So, what can we as parents do to help: The first thing we need to do is encourage our children to experiment with numbers. One way they can experiment at home is to count physical objects. Let them count your forks and spoons as they set the table for dinner. Let them count cans and boxes as they help you put groceries away. If all else fails, let them count M&Ms. Soon they will be ready to replace the physical objects with written numbers and to begin addition and subtraction.

Provide your child with an environment where she can freely explore a wide variety of materials and ask questions about those materials that encourage her to arrive at her own conclusions. You need not purchase anything special. Ask your child *How many pennies are in our penny jar?* and you give her the opportunity to estimate and to count.

In order to help your child understand the language of math, it needs to be presented in a context that makes sense to her. Use her language and her experiences as a starting point to help her develop an understanding of math operations and concepts. Use her toys and household items when creating problems for the games in this section. She needs to be able to see and touch the objects she is counting.

The *What Works* study states, "Children in early grades learn mathematics more effectively when they use physical objects in their lessons." By using objects, your child is able to arrive at an understanding of the concept by seeing it. This is becoming increasingly important as television creates a new generation of visual learners. Children need to see that numbers actually relate to their world for math to begin to make sense. With a kitchen scale and a piece of fruit, your child *sees* pounds. The more time spent with this type of activity, the better she will be able to understand the concepts and the application of otherwise abstract symbols.

As a parent, you can keep your child interested, even if the work is difficult, and you can help your child understand the language of math so she can succeed. Her successes will probably begin at home, but once she grows in confidence, she will carry her new skills into the classroom.

Keep your child's ability level in mind while working with her. You will not be able to force her to understand what is beyond her developmental level. You can, however, expect her to solve problems and to begin to build a mathematical vocabulary through a discussion of what she has actually done. While baking cookies for Cub Scouts, my boys and I had an opportunity to discuss how many cookies would be left over for them once each Scout got two.

The process of exploration is more important than the end product. These math activities are designed to help develop creativity, imagination, and self-esteem in the process of strengthening math skills.

These activities will help your child understand the facts she has memorized and those she will learn later. The games will enable her to apply these facts in the classroom and in life. Through practical investigation, your child will assess information, formulate questions, and attempt to find solutions to mathematical situations. She will be encouraged to acquire and practice her math facts in order to be successful in the activities. The games will provide your child with a positive experience using numbers and will encourage her to want to play with numbers in new and creative ways. She will develop a mathematical confidence that she will carry with her through life. Who knows, eventually, she may figure out how old Matthew's cat is. Have fun trying!

GUESSTIMATION

PURPOSE: This game requires your child to visualize a completed project in order to be able to estimate how it can be done.

MATERIALS NEEDED: Small household objects as your measurer: pencil, bottle cap, paper clip, and the like.

NUMBER OF PLAYERS: 2 to 6.

TIME: Allow 15 to 30 minutes.

SKILLS DEVELOPED: This game encourages curiosity and originality of thinking. Your child must make generalizations based on previous experiences, and he must apply what he already knows to new situations. Once he has measured an object, he will have some idea of the measurement of another object of similar size. He will use his hunches and will need to take risks and guesses. All are important in getting the most out of a math curriculum. A child who is afraid to try a problem for fear of getting it wrong will have a harder time learning math because he will not allow himself to experiment. This game will also show him that there is more than one way to measure objects, because measurement is not used in the traditional sense in this case. He will not be using standard measuring tools such as rulers, yardsticks, or tape measures. Who knows, this could lead to a career in engineering!

HOW TO PLAY: The object of the game is to predict, as closely as possible, the measurement of an object. Choose an item you have around the house—a pencil, a book, a bottle cap—as your measure. One player must pick an object that is larger than the measure, and all players estimate how many of the measures will cover the object. For example: How many bottle caps will it take to cross the television screen? How many pencils will cover the length of the bed? Each player guesses aloud how many of the items will need to be used. Each player uses the same measure to check his estimate and the player who comes closest to the correct number wins.

HINTS AND VARIATIONS: This is a good place for the imagination to take over, and the crazier the task the more fun it will be. Everyone has the same chance of winning as no one could have any idea beforehand, for instance, how many paper clips will cover the width of the sports page of the paper. If the child has difficulty counting, one person, possibly you, could do the counting for everyone. Your child can guess a number and the measuring activity will give that number meaning.

Sometimes we played this game while my boys were in the bathtub. They used the soap, a face cloth, toy boats, anything that was available to measure the bathtub.

WEIGHT A MINUTE

PURPOSE: With this game your child will practice estimating and comparing.

MATERIALS NEEDED: You will need a kitchen scale or a bathroom scale. The other materials are determined by what is available.

NUMBER OF PLAYERS: 2 to 4.

TIME: Allow 10 to 20 minutes.

SKILLS DEVELOPED: This game will give your child a better understanding of the concept of weight because she will be able to experiment by weighing many new items and by comparing them with items she is familiar with. With repeated play, "Weight a Minute" encourages her to estimate the weight of an object based on previous experiences with this game and helps her test the validity of her predictions. The game provides a better understanding of *greater than* and *less than*—concepts emphasized throughout school in math and science classes and on standardized tests.

HOW TO PLAY: The object of the game is to guess the weight of an item. Use whatever is available in your house—apples, a squash, a hammer, nails, paintbrushes. Each player guesses the weight of an object and tells the others what she has guessed. No two players may choose the same weight. The item is then weighed. If it is small, weigh it on the kitchen scale. For larger items—iron skillets, paint cans, a step stool—have your child weigh herself on the bathroom scale, record her weight, and then weigh her holding the item. (You can make your own decision about whether you want to get on the scale yourself.) Subtract her weight from her weight plus the item, and you will have the item's weight. Calculate the difference between the estimated weights and the actual weight. The player who comes closest to the actual weight is the winner.

HINTS AND VARIATIONS: This is a good way to give your child your attention while you are cooking dinner or working on a project around the house. Keep the scale handy and bring it out whenever you want your child to "help" in your activity. If more than two players are playing, you will want to record the guesses to avoid arguments later. When playing with younger children, you will need to do the math computations. Older children might be able to do the math themselves and will get practice in subtracting in the process.

COUNT TO TWENTY

PURPOSE: This game provides practice in counting and encourages strategic thinking and planning.

MATERIALS NEEDED: Game board, markers, and a die.

NUMBER OF PLAYERS: Best with 2.

TIME: Allow 20 to 30 minutes.

SKILLS DEVELOPED: Counting is an important part of your child's math program, and it is always a good idea to practice what he is learning. With this game, your child will count by ones or twos with a goal in mind. If he wants to be the player to reach the goal number, he must use strategy and think ahead to the next turn in order to be successful. As you will see in the How to Play paragraph, he must also be mindful of everyone else's turn and pay close attention to the numbers being used. This is a fast and fun way for him to learn how to use an old skill in a more challenging way.

HOW TO PLAY: The object of the game is to count by alternating with another player and to be the player to arrive at the number 20. The players take turns counting, with the first player beginning with the number 1. Each player may add 1 or 2 (but no more than 2) numbers with each of his turns. For example, the first player says *1*, the next says *2*; the next says *3, 4*; the next says *5*; the next says *6, 7*; and so on until they reach the number 20. The player who says *20* gets to roll the die and move along the game board. The winner is the first player to move all the way around the board.

HINTS AND VARIATIONS: Any number can be the target number, depending on the time you have available and the ages of the players. With older children and lots of time, count to 50. If you use higher numbers as the target number, allow up to three numbers to be used at a time for each turn. With very young children, make 10 the limit.

This game can also be played without the game board and it is a good waiting or car activity. When played without a board, the player to say *20* is the winner. If time allows, play again.

To make the game go faster while using the board, use two dice instead of one. Try playing it a different way each time you play. Change the target number from even to odd, or allow variations in how many numbers may be added during the round. It sounds easy, but takes strategy and planning to win.

I'VE GOT A PROBLEM

PURPOSE: This game encourages your child to pay careful attention to detail, increases her attention span, and motivates her to use her creativity and imagination.

MATERIALS NEEDED: None, but play in an area where there is plenty of activity.

NUMBER OF PLAYERS: 3 or more.

TIME: Allow 10 to 20 minutes.

SKILLS DEVELOPED: Your child will have an easier time in school if she learns to pay attention to detail. There are learning experiences all around us; you want to encourage your child to investigate, experiment, and test what she sees. This is all part of math. If she begins to wonder and develop questions about what she sees, you have opened her eyes to endless possibilities for further exploration. She will also have a better understanding of how to solve her math word problems in school once she has created them herself.

HOW TO PLAY: The object of the game is to create and solve word problems based on what is going on around you. This game is somewhat similar to "Ask Me a Question" in the writing section. Here, however, the players are expected to both create a math problem using what is around them and present it in words to the other players to be solved. An example based on simple observation could be: One waitress is carrying two dishes. Another waitress is carrying three dishes. How many dishes are there all together? A more complex problem might be: Five cars are stopped at the toll booth in front of us. When two get through the booth, how many cars must pay before our turn?

All players except the presenter will try to solve the problem and the one who solves the problem first is the winner and presents the next problem.

HINTS AND VARIATIONS: This is a good game to play at the dinner table or while waiting at a restaurant. I liked to play with my boys while they watched sports on television. It added an educational component to a leisure activity.

Since your child will not always be able to touch the items used to make the problem, allow her to use any materials around her as counters—forks, pencils, napkins—if she needs help in arriving at the answer. Since the skill of making the problem is as important as arriving at the correct answer, be sure to praise your child for her creativity.

WIPE OUT

PURPOSE: This game gives your child practice with number facts while encouraging decision making.

MATERIALS NEEDED: 2 dice.

NUMBER OF PLAYERS: 2 to 4.

TIME: Allow 15 to 20 minutes.

SKILLS DEVELOPED: This game encourages your child to develop a plan of action and to take mathematical risks. It is a fast-moving and entertaining way for your child to practice combining numbers. Making the wrong decision can eliminate him from the game, but he will see that one wrong decision does not take away from the fun of the game or the skill he has gained. Sportsmanship plays a big part in this game and it is a good time for you to emphasize the importance of cooperation and a respect for the rights of others.

HOW TO PLAY: The object of this game is to add the values of the rolls in an attempt to come closest to the number 50 without going over and without rolling "snake eyes" (two 1s). Each player, in turn, rolls the dice as many times as he wants, adding the value of each roll to his last total. He may stop at any number before 50 and name that as his total or try to roll until totals add up to 50. The player to come closest to 50 without going over is the winner. Any player rolling "snake eyes" is wiped out and eliminated from that round of play.

HINTS AND VARIATIONS: With older children, you could raise the goal number to 100 or higher. If you want to encourage the use of multiplication facts, have your child multiply the numbers on the dice by each other before adding that number to the total. You can even start at 50 or 100 and have the players subtract the number on the two dice until he gets to 0.

The ways of combining numbers in this game are open to any creative suggestion your child might have. Encourage him to use his imagination.

HIGH ROLLER

PURPOSE: In this game, your child will practice number facts and develop a stronger understanding of the concepts of greater than and less than.

MATERIALS NEEDED: 3 dice.

NUMBER OF PLAYERS: 2 to 4.

TIME: Allow 15 to 30 minutes.

SKILLS DEVELOPED: This game encourages your child to look at a situation involving a combination of three numbers and to use those numbers to solve a problem. Your child will develop an understanding of the values of numbers in order to select the largest. She will analyze what she sees and execute a plan to reach a goal.

HOW TO PLAY: The object of this game is to create a number that is higher than those of the other players. Each player, in turn, rolls the three dice. She then sets the die with the highest value aside and rolls the remaining two again. The higher valued die is again set aside and the single remaining die is rolled. For example, if the original three dice showed *3, 5, 2,* the *5* would be set aside and the *3* and *2* would be rolled again. The new values on the two dice might be *4* and *1*. The *4* would be set aside and the *1* would be rolled again. That die might show a *2* in the final roll. The three numbers to be combined would be *5, 4, 2*. These are combined, either through addition for younger children or through multiplication for older children, to get a total: *5 + 4 + 2 = 11* or *5 × 4 × 2 = 40*. The player with the highest total wins.

HINTS AND VARIATIONS: This game can be as varied as the abilities of the players. Older children who are learning multiplication facts can be required to multiply the first two numbers and add the third, or add the first two numbers and multiply by the third, or simply use multiplication with all three numbers. You can even try to be the one with the smallest number by using subtraction and division. Try and play a different way each time you play.

With a child who is just beginning to work with numbers, this game provides practice with the concepts of *greater than* and *less than,* as she must always determine which value is higher.

WHAT IS THE NUMBER?

PURPOSE: This game encourages your child to discover creative ways to calculate numbers.

MATERIALS NEEDED: A game board and markers.

NUMBER OF PLAYERS: 2 to 4.

TIME: Allow 20 to 30 minutes.

SKILLS DEVELOPED: This game provides practice in using number facts in different ways and encourages your child to consider many ways to combine numbers. He must find new ways to present a problem when it is his turn to give clues, and when answering, he must be able to apply what he has learned.

In school, your child is always being presented with math problems to be solved and he will have a better understanding of them if he has practice in creating the problems himself. When he sees how problems are developed, he will be better able to rearrange difficult problems in his mind in order to change them into something he can solve. This activity also encourages a high degree of originality.

HOW TO PLAY: The object of the game is to figure out a secret number from clues given as to its value. One player chooses a number that he keeps secret from the other players. He gives the other players mathematical clues to the value of the number. For example, if the secret number is *16,* the clue might be *This number is 4 less than 10 plus 10.* The older the child, the more complex the clues should be.

My niece is in the first grade. When she plays this game she uses much simpler clues, such as *This number is 2 plus 2* for the secret number *4.*

Players advance one space on the game board for each correct answer. If the player cannot figure out the number from the clue, the presenting player moves a space and then provides another clue. The first player around the board wins.

HINTS AND VARIATIONS: The numbers used must be tailored to the ages of the players. Younger players will use lower numbers and clues should involve addition and subtraction operations. Older children might begin to use higher numbers with multiplication clues. Allow the use of calculators if you feel it is appropriate for younger players when playing against older players. This can allow the number combinations to be more complex. Include bonus (move ahead two spaces) and penalty (move back one space) squares to add an element of chance and to create more of a challenge.

FOOD FOR THOUGHT

PURPOSE: This game encourages your child to look closely at numbers and to gain a better understanding of nutritional information.

MATERIALS NEEDED: For this game use packaged food items with nutritional labels.

NUMBER OF PLAYERS: 2 to 6.

TIME: Allow 20 to 30 minutes.

SKILLS DEVELOPED: In this game your child will use addition, subtraction, multiplication, or division to help her learn more about the foods she eats. It is never too early to educate your child about nutrition, and by playing this game she will be practicing math facts (as well as her reading skills) while she is learning more about food values.

HOW TO PLAY: The object of the game is to create and solve problems from information found on boxes or cans of packaged foods in your home. Each player chooses a box or a can and uses the numbers on it to create a math problem: If one serving of peanut butter contains 32 grams, and 9 of these grams are protein, and 5 are carbohydrates, how many grams are left for the other nutrients?

One player writes a problem on a piece of paper and presents it to the other players to solve. The problems can be solved on paper or aloud. The presenting player does not necessarily have to know the answer herself, and answers can be checked by calculator or by you as moderator. The player who solves the problem first gets a point. The person with the most points after every person has presented a problem wins.

HINTS AND VARIATIONS: You might want to give points for the creation of a problem, as that is really the most important part of the game. Play at the breakfast table with a cereal box: If there are 3 grams of sugar and 2 grams of salt in the cereal, how much more sugar than salt is there? Or, you can play while preparing dinner. If you are serving macaroni and cheese and the box states that the ingredients contain 190 calories before the butter and milk are added and 290 calories with the butter and milk, how many calories are in the butter and milk?

When you play at the spur of the moment, don't try to write the problems down. Each person can take a turn giving a problem aloud and the other person can try to solve it as quickly as possible.

My boys tried to get me to buy their favorite junk foods by arguing that there were so many ingredients and additives that they must be good! There are endless possibilities for problems in this game!

COMBOS

PURPOSE: This game provides practice with number facts while reinforcing skills in data collecting, organizing, and recording.

MATERIALS NEEDED: Lined paper, pencils, and 2 dice.

NUMBER OF PLAYERS: 2 to 4.

TIME: Allow 15 to 30 minutes.

SKILLS DEVELOPED: This game encourages logical and sequential thinking. Each player must fill in all spaces on a score card by rolling the dice to obtain those numbers. He must also keep the final goal in mind while he makes progress toward that goal. There may be many turns where your child is unable to score any points at all, and here you can help him learn the value of being a good sport and maintaining a sense of humor. The games show the many different ways to arrive at the same point, so exploration and originality are important.

HOW TO PLAY: The object of the game is to roll the dice to create all number totals between 2 and 12. Each player numbers the lines on his paper from 2 to 12 down one side of the page. He gets one roll of the dice each turn and combines the number values of the dice to determine a total value. For example, if the values on the dice are *2* and *3*, an X will be placed next to the *5* on the paper. The next player then rolls and records his combination on his paper. Each number on the paper must be marked as the combinations are rolled. If the combined values on the dice are the same as ones that have already been marked, the player loses that turn. For example, dice with the values of *1* and *4* cannot be used if the player only has the number *8*

remaining on his paper. Play continues until one player makes all his numbers.

HINTS AND VARIATIONS: To increase the difficulty of this game, require that the numbers be rolled in the numerical order in which they appear on the paper, or that each number must be rolled two or three times. Younger children can be encouraged to use bottle caps or other counters to help them add the numbers together if they are at the beginning stages of learning to add. Allow your child to be as creative as possible in combining the values of the numbers. Dice with a 1 and 4 can be recorded as a 5 by addition, a 4 by multiplication, or a 3 by subtraction.

FIFTY

PURPOSE: In this game your child practices combining numbers with a strategy in mind.

MATERIALS NEEDED: A deck of cards (face cards removed), and a calculator (optional).

NUMBER OF PLAYERS: 2 to 4.

TIME: Allow 10 minutes each round.

SKILLS DEVELOPED: This game will help your child feel more comfortable with numbers and will reinforce her memory of math facts. It will also motivate your child to develop strategies and to take risks with numbers, something many children are afraid to do in school for fear of being wrong.

Each move in this game involves a choice. Your child must carefully observe the cards being played and the strategy of the other players in order to determine which card to use during her turn. The skills developed in "Fifty" can also be applied when learning chess or bridge. Chess and bridge require players to analyze the other players' moves before deciding on a plan of attack or defense.

HOW TO PLAY: The object of the game is to put down the last card that can be played without going over a total of 50 points. One player shuffles the cards and places them in a pile, face down, in the middle of the players. The first player takes two cards from the pile, chooses one, and places it face up in the center of the table. She does not show the other card to the other players. The next player also takes two cards, places one on top of the first card face up, and announces the total value of the numbers on the cards in the pile. Each player continues to draw two cards and uses them with the remaining cards in her hand. She chooses one placing it on the exposed pile and adding the value of her card, until someone reaches 50 exactly or cannot play without going over 50. The winner is the last to play a card without going over 50.

HINTS AND VARIATIONS: When playing with older children, consider using more than one deck and raising the final number above 50. This game can also be played by beginning with the number 50 and subtracting cards until you arrive at 0. Allow players to use a calculator if necessary to make the game go faster, and allow younger children to use bottle caps or other small items as counters. You can add an additional creative element by using the face cards and deciding ahead of time what they will stand for. For example, King = lose one turn; Queen = extra turn; Jack of Spades = instant winner.

COLUMN COUNTER

PURPOSE: This game encourages an appreciation of the concept of larger and smaller numbers.

MATERIALS NEEDED: Paper, pencils, and 2 dice.

NUMBER OF PLAYERS: 2 to 4.

TIME: Allow 10 to 30 minutes for each round.

SKILLS DEVELOPED: Your child needs to practice with the concept of place value in order to work with numbers greater than 9. He needs to know that although 11 is written with two 1s, it is still greater than 9. He will be creating numbers and will develop a better understanding of the values the numbers represent. The game also requires him to make decisions in placing a number in a particular location on a chart and he must accept the consequences of his decision, even if they do not work in his favor. He will need to make predictions about the numbers that will appear on the dice and will be able to immediately test the validity of his predictions. This game could show him the futility of gambling and save him a lot of money in the future!

HOW TO PLAY: The object of the game is to create a number with a value higher than the numbers of the other players. Each player folds a sheet of paper lengthwise into several columns. For younger players, fold the paper into two or three columns. Third graders might be able to work with four or five columns. Each column represents a number place value. The column on the right represents and should be labeled *Ones;* the next is *Tens;* then *Hundreds;* then *Thousands;* and so on. Label all columns at the top of the page. Each player, in turn, rolls the dice and records the total rolled in any one of the empty columns he chooses. Use only place numbers 1 through 9—if the number is higher than 9, roll again. The goal is to have the highest numbers in the columns with the highest values. Once a number is placed in a column, it can't be moved. For example, if a 6 is rolled, you have no way of knowing whether you will roll higher or lower numbers in future turns and you must decide where to place the 6. If you decide to place it in the column with the highest value, you must record your next number (even if it is 8 or 9) in a column of lower values. The rolls continue until all columns are filled for everyone. The player who creates a number with the highest value wins.

A sample column counter might look like this:

Thousands	Hundreds	Tens	Ones

In a sample game, if the first number rolled is 6, your child must decide where to place it. Since the lowest number he could roll is 2 and the largest is 9, 6 is about in the middle. He might place it in the hundreds column:

Thousands	Hundreds	Tens	Ones
	6		

If he rolls 9 on his next turn, he is lucky. Your child knows that is the highest possible number, so he places it in the thousands column:

Thousands	Hundreds	Tens	Ones
9	6		

On his next roll he rolls an 8. Too bad he didn't roll that before he placed the 6 in the hundreds column. He would probably want to place it in the tens column:

Thousands	Hundreds	Tens	Ones
9	6	8	

Your child's final roll is a *3:*

Thousands	Hundreds	Tens	Ones
9	6	8	3

His total is *9,683.*

HINTS AND VARIATIONS: With younger children, you can use bottle caps or small toys in the columns so the child will have a better understanding of the quantity of the numbers and will be able to visualize which number is larger or smaller. Place value is a different concept, so don't be discouraged if your young child does not fully grasp it. If you choose to use rolls of 10 through 12, they can be recorded as follows: 10 = 0; 11 = roll again; 12 = player's choice. Allow your child to make up rules for 10 through 12 to add more variety to the game.

As my boys grew comfortable with this game, they enjoyed making more and more columns. It wasn't long before they understood the value of 1 million.

FOOD SHOPPING

PURPOSE: This game gives your child practice with number facts and problem solving while encouraging her to become an educated consumer.

MATERIALS NEEDED: Grocery ads from local newspapers, paper, and pencils.

NUMBER OF PLAYERS: 2 to 4.

TIME: Allow 15 to 30 minutes.

SKILLS DEVELOPED: It is important for your child to recognize that math has practical applications outside the classroom. With this game, she will need to compare and contrast prices listed and determine the lowest price. She will need to read number information critically and will become aware of how to combine numbers to provide more complete information. She will also need to convince you that her solution to the problem is the best one. This will provide an opportunity to "speak math." Careful here. If your child becomes a good comparison shopper, you may no longer be able to justify buying as many convenience foods!

HOW TO PLAY: The object of the game is to develop the best list of foods for the family to buy at the lowest prices. You set the budget for the game, because you want to buy the items chosen by the winner. Using the supermarket ads, have each player prepare a standard grocery list for one day's meals. This list must represent a balance of food agreed upon ahead of time—meats, vegetables, carbohydrates, and such—according to the tastes of your family members. Use ads from one or more markets, according to how you usually shop. The winner is the one who creates the best list, according to family consensus, at the lowest overall price. The prize for winning should be that the list will be used when shopping.

HINTS AND VARIATIONS: With younger children, use the numbers as they appear in the ads. For older children, you might want to calculate price per ounce in order to discover which store or which brand offers the best price. Use a calculator if necessary. I particularly liked this game as it was a big help in menu planning. It gave me a better idea of the foods my boys wanted to eat. It is best to play the game the day you plan to shop. For younger children, it is hard to wait too long before seeing results.

SLEUTH

PURPOSE: In this game your child is required to think about how numbers fit into categories.

MATERIALS NEEDED: A kitchen timer or a watch with a second hand.

NUMBER OF PLAYERS: 2 to 4.

TIME: Allow 10 to 20 minutes.

SKILLS DEVELOPED: In order to ask questions in this game, your child will have to think about all the things he has learned about numbers and number patterns (odd and even; greater than, less than; counting by twos; and the like). He will have to use that language to help him solve the problems. He will learn that numbers are logical and follow a set pattern, but that numbers can fit into many categories (even numbers are all multiples of 2) and can be used in many ways. "Sleuth" encourages flexible thinking.

HOW TO PLAY: The object of the game is to discover another player's secret number. With 2 players, one thinks of a number, and the other must guess the number by asking yes/no questions. For example: *Is it an odd number? Is it greater than 2? Is it a multiple of 5?* No one may ask *is it 4?* (or 12 or 30 or any specific number) until he has asked at least three other questions in an attempt to guess the number. The winner is the one who guesses the opponent's number in the shortest amount of time. If the time factor creates an unfair advantage for one player, just play for the fun of it without keeping score.

HINTS AND VARIATIONS: When playing with younger children, tailor your questions to be challenging, but not beyond their ability to answer. You can use this as an opportunity to explain the difference between odd and even numbers and to clarify greater than and less than. Your child will use the information he has learned in school in new ways as he attempts to guess your secret number.

If there are more than 2 players, players may guess the secret number after all have asked one question. If a player's guess is incorrect, the next player may ask one question and then guess. Play continues until someone guesses the secret number.

THE $1,000 GAME

PURPOSE: This game provides your child with practice in combining numbers in order to develop her ability and be at ease with them. It also shows how numbers relate to the real world.

MATERIALS NEEDED: Newspaper or magazine ads or catalogues, pencils and paper, and calculator (optional).

NUMBER OF PLAYERS: 2 to 6.

TIME: Allow 15 to 30 minutes.

SKILLS DEVELOPED: Combining numbers (adding, subtracting, multiplying, and dividing) is something your child does each school day, and her ability to work with numbers gives some order to her life.

She will need to work with number combinations throughout school and this type of practice can be done in a fun way, making the learning process easier. This game relates the numbers to real items so that the combinations are relevant to her world. "The $1,000 Game" helps her see why she might need to be involved with numbers even after she graduates from school. Anyone who has ever overdrawn a checking account can understand the value of this lesson.

My boys even developed a better understanding of how the costs of their toys added up over time. (Unfortunately, that didn't mean they wanted fewer toys.)

HOW TO PLAY: The object of the game is to "spend" an agreed-upon amount of money. Make it clear at the beginning that this is a "pretend" game so that your child will not expect to get the items she "buys." Since you are using pretend money, maybe you can pretend to play with the toys at the end of the game. A little play acting might be fun.

Set a maximum dollar goal that is meaningful to your child—$50 for a preschooler to $1,000 for an older child. Players purchase items from a catalogue or from ads in newspapers or magazines. Each player records her purchases and keeps a running total. Players may "buy" only one of each item selected. The winner is the first to spend the amount agreed upon or the one who comes closest without going over.

HINTS AND VARIATIONS: Toy catalogues are fun to use for this activity. You can vary this game by starting with the dollar amount and subtracting each time you "spend" money for an item. When you do it this way, the winner would be the first person to reach 0 or the closest to it.

Use a calculator if necessary to make the game go faster, but be sure to record each transaction on paper to avoid mistakes. The sum of $1,000 is a lot of money to a child, and players may be surprised how difficult it is and how long it takes to "spend" that amount.

VARIATIONS

PURPOSE: This game takes the mystery out of numbers and shows your child that there is more than one way to arrive at a correct answer.

MATERIALS NEEDED: Paper and pencils.

NUMBER OF PLAYERS: 2 to 4.

TIME: Allow 20 to 30 minutes.

SKILLS DEVELOPED: Math problems involve putting numbers together to arrive at one correct answer. This game requires your child to begin with the answer and to create the questions. By creating his own number problems, he will discover the secret of how problems are created and this will help him determine which process to use in solving problems in his schoolwork.

HOW TO PLAY: The object of the game is to create a unique number combination that arrives at an agreed-upon answer. One player presents a number over 10 as the answer. All players must write combinations of numbers that are added, subtracted, multiplied, or divided together to arrive at that answer. They should try to think of as many combinations as possible. For example, if the chosen answer is *36*, possible variations may include *6 + 6 + 6 + 6 + 6 + 6; 40–4;* or *1 × 36*. At the end of three minutes, players compare lists. The winner is the one with the most combinations giving the correct answer.

HINTS AND VARIATIONS: Allow your players to use a calculator to verify answers if necessary. This is a good time to let your child use his toys or game pieces to play around with different combinations

(5 teddy bears = 2 teddy bears + 3 teddy bears). Adjust the number you use for the answer to the age of the child. You can use his homework papers as a guide to determine the highest number he is working with at school.

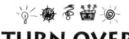

TURN OVER

PURPOSE: In this game your child practices combining numbers and developing decision-making skills.

MATERIALS NEEDED: All of the cards of any one suit from a deck of cards, and 2 dice.

NUMBER OF PLAYERS: 2 to 4.

TIME: Allow 15 to 30 minutes.

SKILLS DEVELOPED: As in "Variations," your child will see that numbers can be made by many different combinations. In this game, she will be limited by the numbers she sees on the dice. She will gain a better understanding of the relationship between different number combinations. She will learn to break down larger numbers into combinations of smaller numbers in order to understand their makeup. This type of activity encourages logical, sequential thinking and helps with determining how to arrive at the answer in word problems. Your child will learn how to take risks in math computation as she sees that there is often not only one right way to arrive at the correct answer. "Turn Over" encourages children to plan ahead and organize.

HOW TO PLAY: The object of the game is to turn over 12 cards in a suit (Ace–Queen). Remove the King and place the cards on the table, face up. Roll the dice. You may turn the corresponding card over for each number on the dice, or you may add the numbers on the dice together and turn over that number card, or you may add the numbers on the dice and turn over two cards that total that number. For this game, Jack = 11 and Queen = 12. Each player rolls the dice and turns over one or more cards to add up to the value of the roll of the dice. For example, if the player rolls *3* and *3* on the dice, she could turn over the *6* card, or the *3, 2,* and *1* cards, or the *5* and *1* cards. The player continues rolling the dice and turning over the cards until she no longer has any cards that correspond to the numbers on the dice. If she rolls a *3* and *4,* but only has a *3* card showing, she cannot make a play. When she can no longer play, she adds the values of the remaining upturned cards. The cards are turned face up again for the next player. She takes her turn and adds the value of the cards remaining. The player with the lowest value of cards remaining is the winner.

HINTS AND VARIATIONS: Children may need help, at first, realizing that they can use different number combinations from those rolled on the dice. You can vary the end result by counting the number of cards remaining and the person with the fewest cards left is the winner. This variation affects the strategy used while playing. If you add the values, the goal will be to turn over the higher value cards first. If you total the cards remaining, the goal will be to turn over as many cards as possible.

With up to four players, each player could play with a different suit.

YOUR NUMBER'S UP

PURPOSE: This game encourages your child to discover ways to solve problems creatively.

MATERIALS NEEDED: A deck of cards.

NUMBER OF PLAYERS: 2 to 4.

TIME: Allow 15 to 30 minutes.

SKILLS DEVELOPED: Your child will be practicing his addition facts while trying to arrive at a creative solution to the problems presented in this game. He will also develop his own problems and learn to reason out problems more easily as he begins to understand the concept of addition. In "Your Number's Up," your child uses card values in different combinations to reach a specific goal. By choosing a different "answer" each time you play, you help your child work with and remember his number facts.

HOW TO PLAY: The object of the game is to create the most problems or "books" for a given answer. All players decide on the goal answer between 11 and 14. One player deals everyone 10 cards, which are kept secret from all the other players. Each card has its number value, ace =1 and face cards = 10. The remaining cards are placed face down in a pile, with one card face up next to it. The first player draws a card. He may select the face-up card or draw from the pile. He groups into small piles (books) any two or more numbers from his hand that equal the goal answer and sets them aside. For example, if the goal is *12,* the player would make books of card values that add up to 12: *2* plus *10; 5* and *7; 3, 1,* and *8.* Each card may only be used one time. After making all combinations possible in the hand, the player must discard one card onto the face-up pile. Play continues with each player, in turn, drawing from either pile, making books, and discarding. If at any time a player runs out of cards before the cards in the face-down pile are gone, he must draw three cards from that pile and begin again. When all of the cards in the face-down pile are gone, the player with the most books wins.

HINTS AND VARIATIONS: Allow as many creative variations as your child might discover. As my children got older, they liked to play this game with multiplication combinations and they set a higher goal number. Remember that the goal is to get him to think, not to win. You might award additional points for creative alternatives. The joker may be used as a wild card.

SECRET SQUARE

PURPOSE: This game involves practice with graphs and shows your child that graphs can be fun.

MATERIALS NEEDED: Large square graph paper or paper on which you have drawn grids, paper, and pencils.

NUMBER OF PLAYERS: 2.

TIME: Allow 20 to 30 minutes.

SKILLS DEVELOPED: The ability to read charts and graphs is an important part of math classes as your child gets into middle and high school, and "Secret Square" will help get your child ready. This game requires her to create a graph and use the coordinates to solve a problem. Making a graph and filling it herself will help her understand information she sees in graph form. Points on a graph are named by the letters going down the side and the numbers going across the top. She has to be alert to all possible combinations of numbers and letters on the graph in order to use as many of the combinations as she needs. She has to use trial and error and experimentation in order to solve the problem.

HOW TO PLAY: The object of the game is to locate the other player's secret square by using the points on a graph. Only 2 players can play this at a time. Each player numbers the squares across the top of her graph and puts letters in each square going down the side of the graph. She then makes an *X* or draws an object in a secret square on her own graph.

	1	2	3	4	5	6	7	8	9	10
A										
B										
C										
D										
E										
F										
G			X							
H										
I										
J										

The players, in turn, call off the letter and number that represents a particular square on the graph in an attempt to locate the other player's *X*. For example, a square in the middle of the graph would be at the point where the letter *G* and the number *4* would cross if each were extended into the graph. As each player guesses a coordinate, she blackens in that square on her own graph so she will remember which squares she has already guessed. Play continues until one player has located the secret square of the other player and that player is the winner. This is a peacetime version of the game Battleship.

HINTS AND VARIATIONS: This game is best suited to 2 players, but younger children could pair up with older children or an adult. You might want to work in pairs with your child for the first time, so that she can learn how to play from your example. The game is not as difficult as it might appear. Encourage your child to use her finger as a guide in naming the coordinates of the square. Starting at a number, move your finger down to any square you choose. Then move your finger to the letter at the side that is on that line. That number and letter are the name of the square.

My boys enjoyed drawing objects (a soccerball, an animal, a smiley face) instead of an *X* in the secret square.

ORDER

PURPOSE: This game provides practice with addition, subtraction, multiplication, and division while encouraging organizational skills and strategical planning.

MATERIALS NEEDED: Paper, pencils, and 3 dice.

NUMBER OF PLAYERS: 2 to 4.

TIME: Allow 15 to 30 minutes.

SKILLS DEVELOPED: Your child has to be alert to all combining possibilities of numbers that appear on the dice. He must use his roll to his best advantage, and this involves strategy. He must work in a logical and sequential manner and must determine the best mathematical process to use in a given situation. This is the skill needed when working with number problems in school.

If Ethan is 5 feet tall and is 2 inches taller than Aaron, and Aaron is 4 inches shorter than Katie, how tall is Katie?

In order to solve this type of problem, your child will need to work in an organized way. Before he can begin to solve the problem, he must develop a strategy for solving it.

HOW TO PLAY: The object of the game is to roll all the numbers from 1 to 12 in order. This is accomplished by rolling the actual numbers or by combining any of the numbers rolled. The numbers must be rolled in order and a 1 must be rolled before any other number can be recorded. Each player writes 1 through 12 down the side of his paper. Then the players, in turn, roll the 3 dice and check off the number or numbers they can make by adding them together. For example, a roll of *1, 2,* and *3* on the dice could be counted as *1, 2,* and *3;* or as *4* (3+1); or *5* (3+2); or *6* (3+2+1); depending on the number needed to complete the sequence. When combining numbers, not all of the dice need to be used. A player continues his turn as long as he is able to check off a number he needs. When he misses, and can do nothing with his roll, the next player rolls the dice. The winner is the first player to roll all of the numbers.

HINTS AND VARIATIONS: Allow your child to use any process—addition, subtraction, multiplication, division—that will arrive at a desired number. The thinking that must go into arriving at the best answer is just as important as the answer, but use calculators and counters if necessary. You can increase the challenge for older players by requiring all players to go from 1 to 12 and then from 12 to 1. This game is similar to "Combos" but encourages a different way of thinking. Numbers must be rolled in order, and the use of 3 dice increases the ways the numbers can be combined. It is more difficult than "Combos" and might not be as appropriate for younger children.

This is a good way to encourage the use of multiplication with older children. For example, the numbers *1, 2,* and *3* could be combined: $1 + 2 = 3 \times 3 = 9$.

FOUR

WHAT?

Helping Your Child
Develop Memory Strategies

What is your best friend's phone number? When is your mother-in-law's birthday? What did the neighborhood you grew up in look like? Can you name the Great Lakes? When you answer these questions, you are using memory strategies you have learned over the years. Perhaps the repetition of dialing your friend's phone number has helped you memorize it. Maybe you keep a list of important birthdates written on your calendar. When you think about your old neighborhood, you probably create a picture of it in your mind. If your teacher taught you to use the acronym HOMES to remember the names of the Great Lakes, you use a mnemonic device. All these strategies help you remember.

The development of strong memory strategies will help your child, too. Whether they help him remember the name of a playmate in nursery school, or the names of the presidents, these skills are essential. Unfortunately, though most everything your child will learn in school is related to memory, little time is spent developing memory strategies.

What can we do to help? We can expose our children to strategies to help strengthen their memories. We can demonstrate how repetition will help them memorize information and how categorizing information might be more helpful. Sometimes it is easier to remember when the information is divided into manageable "chunks." Often, writing down information or drawing pictures of the information can assist memory. When children can visualize what they are trying to remember, recall is even more accurate.

The games in this section are designed to strengthen your child's memory skills. They give children practice in many of the strategies that will help them remember important information. Memory skills help children learn to spell; they help them with reading comprehension and math facts; they help them learn important dates and facts from history; and they will help them achieve higher level thinking skills.

Repetition is an elementary strategy that even very young children can use. When young children learn to talk, they mimic your expressions and learn new words by repeating yours. Repeating spelling words can help them remember. Though repetition is limited in its usefulness, it is appropriate for some learning situations, such as practicing the multiplication tables.

Children use chunking and categorization strategies to remember longer and more complicated information. They may break the information down into manageable sections. Young children use this chunking strategy to learn the alphabet with The Alphabet Song. The information is broken down into smaller, more memorable parts—ABCD EFG HIJK LMNOP. . . . Often, they remember phone numbers the same way, the first three numbers, then the last four. Older children can chunk sections of social studies assignments. Rather than trying to remember everything about India in one session, they may divide the information into sections, then attack each chunk individually—climate, holidays, government, etc. Once they have mastered each individual chunk, they can add the next until they have learned and remembered all the information.

When children learn to categorize information, they not only improve their memory, but they begin to make abstract associations that enhance their thinking skills. At an early level, this type of strategy helps children separate numbers from letters. Later, it will help children separate information, such as animals that live in the water and animals that live on land. At a more advanced level, this strategy helps children see similarities and differences in order to integrate new information with information they have already stored.

The most sophisticated and the most important memory strategy is visualization. Visualization helps improve memory in all areas—if a child can visualize something, he can remember it. When children visualize, they make pictures in their minds of what they would like to remember. Think of their visual memory as a videocassette tape that can be replayed over and over when they need to retrieve information.

Barbara Wilson, the creator of the *Wilson Reading System*, uses visualization strategies to help children remember what they have read. She encourages students to visualize information as they read it or hear it and to create pictures of that information. Children then replay their visual images to solidify the pictures in their memories. She then has children "retell" what they see in their pictures, and this three-step process helps improve listening skills, reading comprehension, and memory.

Visualization is not easy for most children. Living in a world where so much information is already provided in a visual format makes it difficult for children to create images in their minds. Children who spend hours in front of the television, or who read only illustrated books, lose the ability to visualize. Pictures are so often provided for them, that they simply don't know how to go about creating pictures in their minds. However, with practice, children can learn this important skill.

The games in this book encourage children to create their own images and to replay those images in order to remember information. (In addition to these games, you might read aloud books without pictures to your children, or you might begin listening to old radio programs. This will provide children with the opportunity to create strong images in their minds.)

All of the memory games in this section encourage children to organize their thoughts. This type of organized thinking helps children at all levels of development. So, unplug the TV, turn off the computer, and get ready to charge those memory cells. Before you know it, your child might be the next champion on *Jeopardy*.

MIMIC

PURPOSE: This game helps improve visual memory.

MATERIALS NEEDED: None.

NUMBER OF PLAYERS: 2 to 4.

TIME: About 5 minutes for each round.

SKILLS DEVELOPED: This game will help your child focus her attention on a visual image in order to hold that image in her mind. As she mimics the pattern of movements, she uses the strategy of motor movement to improve her visual memory. Perhaps you have used a string tied around a finger to help you remember to do something. This act of tying the string helped you remember what to do.

Children can use visual sequential memory skills to remember spelling words, lists of facts, dates in history, a series of directions, etc. Outside the classroom, experience with this type of visual memory game can help a child on the athletic field. Children need a strong visual memory to recall plays and to adjust their positions in response to changes in the game.

HOW TO PLAY: The object of the game is to recall and mimic a series of movements. The first player strikes a pose. The next player recreates the original pose and follows it with another movement. The following player recreates the original two movements and adds a third, and so on. For example, the first player might twist her body. The second player would twist his body, then reach into the air. The third player would twist her body, reach into the air, then cross her arms. The combinations are endless. The last player who can remember and mimic all the movements wins. Play rotates.

HINTS AND VARIATIONS: This is a good game for young children as it does not involve reading, writing, or language in order to play. It may be played both indoors and outdoors. Players could make their movements very small while playing in the back seat of a car. They could even limit their movements to their fingers or their hands.

In an outdoor setting, movements can be much larger. Giggles are sure to develop while playing this game.

CLAPPER

PURPOSE: This game enhances the ability to recall specific sound patterns.

MATERIALS NEEDED: None.

NUMBER OF PLAYERS: 2.

TIME: 10 minutes or less.

SKILLS DEVELOPED: This game gives your child practice in listening and following directions. Both the player who comes up with the clapping patterns and the player who must repeat them must remember the sequence. Children need sequential memory in order to follow directions, to recall a series of events, to remember their math facts and spelling words, and many other activities that take place in the school environment. Although this game is based on a sound pattern, players are watching the "clapper's" hands. This shows that it is easier to remember things when you hear them *and* see them at the same time.

HOW TO PLAY: One player claps his hands in a specific pattern. For example: Clapping *shave and a haircut, two bits*; a football cheer; or the pattern of a recognizable television or radio commercial. The other player must repeat the pattern, exactly. Play continues until one of the players is unable to repeat the pattern.

HINTS AND VARIATIONS: As the players become more experienced with this game, they will be able to create their own rhythmic patterns. Older players will be able to come up with complex variations. This can be difficult, as the player must remember what she created. Don' t be afraid to stamp your feet as well.

Children who enjoy this game might like to learn more about Morse code.

THE SHELL GAME

PURPOSE: The purpose of this game is to help your child revisualize something he has already seen.

MATERIALS NEEDED: Shells of various shapes and sizes and a blindfold.

NUMBER OF PLAYERS: At least 2 children and 1 parent.

TIME: 10 minutes.

SKILLS DEVELOPED: When your child can produce a mental image of something he has seen, it helps him remember. This is particularly helpful when children are trying to remember information presented in a visual format—filmstrips, videos, slides, etc. This type of memory strategy is also useful when children are trying to learn spelling words or math facts. Once children are old enough to take notes, this type of memory skill can actually help them visualize and remember their notes.

The Shell Game also helps children notice differences. This type of visual discrimination assists them when they are trying to learn shapes, letters, or numbers. Children with strong visual discrimination skills have little trouble seeing the difference between an octopus and a squid, an African and an Asian elephant, or an octagon and a hexagon, for example.

HOW TO PLAY: In this game, parents act as supervisors, rather than participants. The parent presents a selection of shells—some scalloped shaped, some snail shaped, some crab shells, some whelks, and so on Have the children spend 2 minutes studying the shells. Allow the children to touch them or draw pictures of them, if that helps. Blindfold the first player. Have him sort the shells according to shape while blindfolded. Each player takes a turn sorting the shells. Children love the idea of doing things blindfolded, and this game helps them visualize and remember.

Most often, this is a game without winners or losers. It is just fun to play.

HINTS AND VARIATIONS: If you do not live in an area where shells are readily available, play this game with buttons, beads, rocks, beans, or pasta. When the items are most similar, the game is the most difficult. For example, ziti pasta and rigatoni pasta are much the same. The differences will be subtle.

THE LAST WORD

PURPOSE: This game helps children retrieve information by grouping words into categories.

MATERIALS NEEDED: None.

NUMBER OF PLAYERS: 2 or more.

TIME: 1 to 2 minutes for each round.

SKILLS DEVELOPED: With practice, your child can strengthen her ability to recall specific information quickly. Many classroom situations require children to come up with a quick answer to a question. Some children do this with little effort. Others can benefit from strategies to help them recall. The strategy developed here is categorization.

Categorization is a storage technique. When children learn to store information in their brains by categories, it is easier for them to recall and cross-reference the information when they need it. Just about everything can fit into one or more categories. Practice in categorizing improves memory because it helps them find the word they need to recall by finding it within its category.

HOW TO PLAY: The first player chooses a category and names any item that fits into that category. For example, a player might choose to play by naming a fruit. Each player in turn must think of a word that fits the category. Play continues around until no one can think of a word that fits. The winner is the player who comes up with the last word. At the beginning of each round, a new player selects the category—transportation, colors, animals, etc.

HINTS AND VARIATIONS: Another way of playing this game is to use beginning sounds—cat, car, cantaloupe, etc. When children play this game with any word that begins with the same sound, they also work on their pre-reading skills. This variation is similar to "Beginnings" in chapter 1. The emphasis here, however, is on categorization skills rather than reading skills.

THE GATHERER

PURPOSE: This game also provides practice in categorizing.

MATERIALS NEEDED: A tray, or any flat, moveable surface, assorted small objects, a timer or watch with a second hand, and paper and pencils.

NUMBER OF PLAYERS: At least 3.

TIME: Allow 10 minutes for each round.

SKILLS DEVELOPED: The ability to categorize will help your child understand language. When children can categorize, they can apply general information to a specific item. For example, when reading a story about zebras, it is helpful if the child already knows that a zebra is a mammal. That knowledge provides them with information that may not be specifically mentioned in the plot of the story. This type of information helps children make generalizations.

The ability to categorize helps children store and retrieve information. Once the information is placed in categories, it is much easier to recall the information rather than trying to recall a long list of facts. The child who can break down a geography lesson into the categories of climate, economy, history, and customs will be able to recall much more about a country than the child who simply tries to remember facts. In order to play this game, one player must gather a group of objects, and the other players must remember the objects. As the "gatherer" fits objects into categories, his categorization skills are reinforced. As the other players recall the items, the ability to break the objects down into categories will help them remember.

HOW TO PLAY: Each player takes a turn collecting the objects to be used in the game. As the gatherer collects objects, he tries to gather items that fit into several categories. For example: items made of plastic, items that are round, items made of wood. The gatherer places all the items on the tray and allows the other players to look at the tray for 2 minutes. The gatherer takes the tray out of the room, and the players list all the items they can remember. The player who remembers the largest number of items wins. Each player should have a turn to be the gatherer.

HINTS AND VARIATIONS: Younger children could play this game without writing down the objects. They could take turns naming an object on the tray. The last player to name an item on the tray would win. The number of items should vary according to the age of the players. Younger players might play with a few items, all from the same category. Older players may play with many more items and with a larger number of categories. As the parent, you can determine the number of items necessary to play in order to keep the game at the appropriate level for your child.

If there are only 2 players, the game could be played in a slightly different way. Instead of naming all the items on the tray, this game can also be played with a missing item. The gatherer would show all the items to the other player, take the tray out of sight, remove one of the objects, and then bring the tray back to the room. The other player would try to identify the missing item. Or, the pieces on the tray could be rearranged, and the player would have to put the game pieces back in the original order. The roll of gatherer and player should rotate.

TRIPPER

PURPOSE: This is another game to enhance memory and visualization skills.

MATERIALS NEEDED: None.

NUMBER OF PLAYERS: 2 or more.

TIME: 5 to 10 minutes.

SKILLS DEVELOPED: This game provides practice using order as a strategy to help remember. It also fosters creativity and humor. As the child travels through the alphabet, she learns to remember information in a specific order—in this case alphabetically. This enhances sequential memory. This type of activity also helps your child learn to use mnemonic devices to help her remember. Remember when you used the mnemonic device "HOMES" to remember the names of the Great Lakes (Huron, Ontario, Michigan, Erie, Superior). Giving your child the opportunity to practice this type of memory strategy will help her when she needs to remember specific information. Some children use these strategies naturally. Children who have never thought to use this type of strategy can be taught.

HOW TO PLAY: You have probably played some version of this game yourself, without even thinking about the memory activity involved. The first person uses a destination and an item that begins with the letter "A." For example I'm going to ALABAMA, and I'm going to take an APPLE. The next player moves forward one letter in the alphabet for his destination: I'm going to BOSTON and I'm going to take an APPLE and a BOOKBAG. The next player's destination begins with the next letter in the alphabet: I'm going to CALCUTTA and I'm going to take an APPLE, a BOOKBAG, and a CALCULA-TOR. The more outrageous the destinations and the items, the more fun the game. Players are eliminated when they are unable to remember where they are going or what they are going to take. Play continues until there is only one player left, or until you get to the letter "Z." When play continues all the way through the alphabet, all players win.

HINTS AND VARIATIONS: With younger players, you could use an alphabet strip to help them remember the letters. If the alphabet is too long for them, choose one of the player's names for the game. For example: Muffy. I'm going to MARYLAND, and I'm going to take a MINIBIKE. I'm going to UTAH and I'm going to take a MINIBIKE and a UKULELE. Older players will use more sophisticated destinations and objects.

SNAPSHOT

PURPOSE: This game helps develop and improve visual memory and provides practice in recreating visual images.

MATERIALS NEEDED: Photographs or pictures from magazines, paper, pens, pencils, or crayons. A watch with a second hand or a timer.

NUMBER OF PLAYERS: At least 3. The more the merrier.

TIME: Allow 5 to 10 minutes for each round.

SKILLS DEVELOPED: This game encourages players to develop visual awareness, and it helps them develop strategies to improve memory. It may also help them focus on details. In order to play, your child must first hold a total picture in his mind. Then, he will focus on the individual items within the photograph or picture in order to make a drawing of each of the items.

When children have strong visualization skills, they can use visual images to help them remember classroom presentations as well as information provided in filmstrips or videos. Once they record those images, either with notes, or with pictures, their memory of the subject is stronger.

HOW TO PLAY: The object of the game is to remember as many individual items as possible from the presented picture. One player chooses a photograph or picture from a magazine that includes many related or unrelated items. For example, a picture of a farm might be appropriate for young players. Older players might try to remember a picture of a sporting event. The player who chooses the picture acts as timekeeper. All other players study the picture for 1 minute. At the end of the minute, the timekeeper puts the picture away, and the players each try to draw a picture of as many of the items as they can remember in 2 minutes (any close approximation of the item should be accepted). The player who remembers the most items from the picture wins.

HINTS AND VARIATIONS: As players get more experienced at this game, reduce the amount of time they have to study the picture. If the children are intimidated by drawing and are old enough to write, they could list the items they remember. If you select this option, reduce the amount of time they have to recall the picture.

If children are having difficulty remembering more than several items each time, help them to develop memory strategies. They might start by remembering everything of the same color, then everything that is soft, or everything that is hard, or anything that belongs in any particular category. This categorization skill will help them with other memory tasks.

COMMANDO

PURPOSE: This game provides practice in remembering a series of verbal directions.

MATERIALS NEEDED: Pencil and paper.

NUMBER OF PLAYERS: At least 3.

TIME: This one moves very quickly.

SKILLS DEVELOPED: All school age children need to be able to follow directions. When children have difficulty with schoolwork, it is often because they did not follow directions. This game provides practice in listening to a series of commands, visualizing the sequence of the actions required, and executing the tasks. Children will realize that following directions in school is not really that difficult and can even be fun.

HOW TO PLAY: One player writes a series of activities to be completed. For example: touch your nose, hop on your right foot, wink your left eye, then turn in a circle. That player reads the directions to the other players. The directions cannot be repeated. The other players then try to act out the sequence of activities in the correct order. Each player who performs all of the activities in the correct order receives a point. Play rotates and each player has a turn to be the "Commando." The player with the most points at the end of the allotted time wins. Ties are encouraged.

HINTS AND VARIATIONS: The activities should be simple or complex, depending on the age of the players Younger players might only be able to remember two or three simple activities. Older players might choose to perform up to ten. Older players may make their series of activities include finding a passage in a book, reading it aloud, and then acting it out. Encourage them to use their imaginations. When parents play, the list might include: take out the trash, put a new liner in the trash can, empty the dishwasher, and hang up your coat. However, with these activities, parents won't be invited to play too often.

FAMOUS FOLKS

PURPOSE: This game helps children remember visual details and in the process introduces them to world leaders.

MATERIALS NEEDED: Photos of people from newspapers or magazines (you can even use family photos), masking tape, scissors, and a pen.

NUMBER OF PLAYERS: 3 or more.

TIME: Allow 10 to 15 minutes to play, plus additional preparation time.

SKILLS DEVELOPED: Children today are exposed to thousands of visual images over the course of a week. These images are flashed on the television screen for seconds at a time, leaving children no time to appreciate differences and details. This game enhances visual discrimination skills. Children must learn to discriminate in order to recognize countries on a map, to identify a particular species of animal or plant, to recognize people, and even to recognize characters in a picture book. As children practice these discrimination skills, the ability to remember visual details improves.

HOW TO PLAY: You will need some advance preparation to play this game. Someone needs to take the time to collect the photos and to label them. One player collects photos of important world leaders from newspapers or magazines and identifies the person by writing his or her name on the back of the photograph. If there is print on the back of the photograph, simply place a piece of masking tape on the back of the photo and then record the name. This preparation is a perfect rainy day activity.

To begin the game, the person who has collected the photos spreads them out in front of the other players and identifies the individuals in the pictures. Each name is said once. Then, the pictures are scrambled. Each player, in turn, selects a photo, identifies the person, confirms the answer by reading the name aloud from the back of the card, and then places the photo in his or her pile. If the player has made an incorrect guess, he reads the correct name and returns the photo to the game. Play continues until there are no photos left or until everyone is stumped. The player with the most pictures wins. It is fun to play several rounds of this game using the same photos to give the players an opportunity to remember all of the individuals in the photographs.

HINTS AND VARIATIONS: Use the age and experience of your children to determine how many photos to use. When playing with younger children, introduce them to just a few new faces each time. You could start with the President of the United States, the Vice President, and the Attorney General. Each time you play the game, leave some of the individuals they recognize, and add some new leaders. The game may also be played with sports heroes, or the characters from a favorite television program. With older children, use more photographs and less recognizable world leaders. This is supposed to be fun, so be sure there are always some people in the game your children can immediately identify. You can also use this game to help children remember those relatives they don't often see. Photos of Uncle John, Aunt Jarah, and cousins Amy and Ben can be used to help refresh your child's memory before going to a family reunion. If necessary, you can give the children tricks to help them remember. For example, Bow Tie Ben, or Jeweled Jarah.

CHUCKY'S CHALLENGE

PURPOSE: This game helps children develop categorization skills while improving visual memory.

MATERIALS NEEDED: Index cards, art supplies and/or pictures from magazines.

NUMBER OF PLAYERS: 2 to 4.

TIME: Allow 15 minutes or more.

SKILLS DEVELOPED: The commercial game of Concentration is an excellent choice for improving visual memory skills, but this game takes it a step further. As with the commercial game, players must remember where a particular card is located. But here, as children try to make category matches, instead of exact matches, they are challenged to think of objects that belong together. This ability to categorize helps even when children are learning to read. They must know the difference between numbers and letters before they can master reading skills. As they get older, the ability to group information makes studying easier.

As children are involved in creating the game pieces, they must come up with objects that fall into particular categories. The process of making the game pieces is just plain fun.

HOW TO PLAY: First, you and your child create the game pieces. You may draw objects on the index cards, or you may cut pictures from magazines and paste them on the cards. As participants are drawing or pasting, they must remember to find two objects that fall into the same category. For example: an apple and a banana; a car and a plane; a parrot and a toucan. With younger children, you may need to help them create the game pieces.

To begin the game, the players shuffle the index cards and place them face down on the floor or on a table. The first player turns over two cards. If they do not belong in the same category, the player returns them to the same spot, face down. The next player turns over one card and decides if the object on the card falls into the same category as one of the previous player's cards. If it does, he tries to remember the position of the first player's card in order to make a category match. If he is successful, he removes the category matches from the game and puts them in his pile. If the card he turns over does not fall into the same category as any of the previous cards, he turns another card over at random. If the objects match, he removes the cards to his pile. If they don't match, he returns them to the original position. As play continues, more and more objects are exposed, and the players have a greater chance of making matches if they are able to remember where the objects are located. The player who has found the most category matches at the end of the game wins.

HINTS AND VARIATIONS: The level of difficulty in this game can be adjusted by the number of cards in play. The more cards, the more difficult the game. With younger players, start with 10 cards and increase the number as the children become more experienced. Older players can play with up to 50 cards.

On occasion, players will select objects that could fall into more than one category. For example, four objects could be a car, a train, a plane, and a cloud. The player who created the matches intended the plane to match the cloud as an object in the sky, but the player who turned over the plane matched it to a train as a type of transportation. When this happens, if the player can justify his match, she claims the match. The ability to explain how the two objects go together is enhanced when children must come up with reasons for their matches. When this happens, the game may end with some unmatched cards.

FIVE

INVOLVING OLDER
CHILDREN

Those of us with more than one child know how difficult it can sometimes be to have them play cooperatively. The immediate response when suggesting that older and younger sisters and brothers play together is usually, "No way!" When I first suggested my sons play these games together, that was exactly the response I got. My boys are only two years apart, and when they were younger they would rather fight than eat. In talking with friends whose children were closer in age or farther apart, I found my problem was not unique.

At almost any age, your child is fighting for your attention, and his greatest rival is usually a brother or a sister. In some families this does not present a problem—it did in mine. I was constantly playing the role of referee for my two boys, and there was usually a great deal of tension when they were together. My creativity was stretched to the limit simply trying to come up with ways to keep them from hurting each other, physically and verbally. Although these games cannot work miracles, they do provide an opportunity for healthy competition among brothers and sisters and a chance for each child to be recognized for his accomplishments.

Family game times can be fun, but they do require some planning. In order to encourage family game time when ability levels are vastly different, it is important to encourage your older child to be your ally. You might want to have a "secret pact" with the older one to be a "helper" with the younger one. This provides a chance for an older child to be a teacher and a positive role model. This puts him in a most favorable position. He gains your respect and approval in his role as ally, and he has the opportunity to share his knowledge and expertise with a younger brother or sister. What a boost to his self-esteem!

The Hints and Variations sections of most of the games in this book offer suggestions for playing in teams. You can team with the younger child against the older one, or if you are trying to encourage your children to be more cooperative with each other, have them team up against you. This way, everybody wins.

While helping the younger sibling develop and strengthen his skills, the older one will be learning something from the games in spite of himself. Since there is rarely only one correct answer, he is not limited to a specific way to solve a problem. The games encourage him to stretch his imagination, take risks in solving problems, and challenge himself.

Of course, this idea of involving your younger and older children cooperatively will not always work. In that case, accept their differences and try again another time, or with another game.

Another alternative is to offer your older child a game time of his own as a bonus after your younger child has gone to bed. Parents sometimes forget that older siblings enjoy playing with their parents and having some of their undivided attention. The following games were created to help you get involved with your older children as well. These games enhance thinking skills in upper elementary age children by using materials that are more appropriate to their developmental levels. And, when your older child sees how much fun these games can be, he might be more receptive to playing the other games with you and your younger child.

READING GAMES

YELLOW PAGES

PURPOSE: This game reinforces research skills and helps children read for detail.

MATERIALS NEEDED: The yellow pages of a phone book, and a kitchen timer. Borrow extra yellow pages from friends, since this game is enhanced when everyone has a copy to work with.

NUMBER OF PLAYERS: 2 or more.

TIME: Allow 5 minutes per round.

SKILLS DEVELOPED: As your child gets into middle school and high school, she will be expected to do more and more research. All of those alphabetical skills she is now learning in elementary school will later have to be used for locating information quickly in reference books. She will also be expected to pick out the important information from materials provided. The more familiar she is with this process, the more comfortable she will be when she needs to find information quickly to present in class or to use in a project. The process of locating information is a skill that can be taught.

HOW TO PLAY: The object of the game is to locate specific information in the yellow pages of a phone book. One player asks for information that the other player must find in the yellow pages. Tasks might include, *Find a service station that will tow,* or *Find a pizza restaurant that delivers.* The next player must then locate the information in the phone book and show the information she found. Use the timer to see how long it takes for the player to find the entry. That player then asks a question and the other player is timed. The one who finds the entry in the shortest amount of time is the winner. If the time factor creates an unfair advantage for one player, play this game just for the fun of it without keeping score.

My boys once challenged me to find the closest Weight Watcher's clinic. Was that a hint?

HINTS AND VARIATIONS: Do not be concerned if the request is not worded exactly the same as the category found in the phone book. If asked to find a gas station that tows, your child will have to use some additional skills involving cross-referencing to find the right word for the entry. It might be a good idea to go over some of the categories in the phone book before playing because most school-aged children are not in the habit of using the phone book at all, much less the yellow pages. If you are playing with more than 2 players, each player presents her request to the person on her right, and the one who finds her answer first is the winner. (You will, of course, need a phone book for each player for this variation.)

TRIVIA

PURPOSE: This game encourages the use of reference materials and provides practice in skimming skills.

MATERIALS NEEDED: Any kind of almanac, game board, markers, and a timer.

NUMBER OF PLAYERS: 2 or more.

TIME: Allow 15 to 30 minutes for each round.

SKILLS DEVELOPED: In the upper grades of elementary school, the ability to use reference materials is very important, as is the ability to determine which type of materials to use for a specific task. Most school children are not familiar with almanacs and don't know how much information is available in them. This game gives your child practice in using an almanac, a book he will be able to use in projects and report writing in school. Any time you can widen the scope of his information about the resources available, take advantage of the opportunity.

HOW TO PLAY: The object of the game is to locate specific information in an almanac. One player browses in the almanac, finding bits of information he thinks the other players will not know. He asks a question about that information. For example, *What is the capitol of Georgia? What is the state flower of Arkansas?* or *Who won the World Series in 1970?* If the other player can guess the answer correctly, he can move 2 spaces on the game board. If he does not know the answer, he must look it up in the almanac. If he finds the information in under 2 minutes, he moves along 1 space. If he cannot find the answer in the allotted time, the player who presented the question gets to move 1 space. The player to circle the board first is the winner.

HINTS AND VARIATIONS: You might want to adjust the amount of time allowed to find the answer. If you find your child is not able to find answers in 2 minutes, adjust the time accordingly. Don't discourage him from reading because it takes too long.

If your child finds the answers in well under 2 minutes, adjust the limit to 1 minute. Because trivia games are so popular, this game will appeal to your older child because it will increase his store of trivial information. He will be able to stun his friends when he plays trivia-related games.

WRITING GAMES

POLITICS

PURPOSE: This game encourages your child to analyze a picture and choose appropriate words to describe what she sees.

MATERIALS NEEDED: Political cartoons, paper, and pencils.

NUMBER OF PLAYERS: 2 to 6.

TIME: Allow 15 to 30 minutes.

SKILLS DEVELOPED: Report writing in the upper grades requires your child to understand a subject, develop opinions about it, analyze those opinions, and come to some conclusions. This game, on a much smaller scale, calls on those same skills. Your child will have to look at a picture, get meaning from what she sees, analyze the situation presented, and make some judgments. She then will have to write words to support her opinions and may also have to convince the other players that her judgment is correct.

HOW TO PLAY: The object of the game is to list words describing a political cartoon. All players look at the same cartoon; then each player lists words that suggest the emotions or ideas she felt were expressed in the cartoon. For example, a cartoon about a political election might make you think of words such as *decisions, confusion, political, democratic* and the like. When all lists are complete, players read the words they have written and all words that are on more than one list are eliminated. Players receive 1 point for each word that is not on any other list. If a word is challenged by the other players as not being appropriate to the cartoon, the player who used it must defend her choice to the satisfaction of the other players. The player with the most points wins.

HINTS AND VARIATIONS: Save political cartoons from newspapers for several days in order to play for more than one round. It is a good idea to have enough cartoons in order for all the players to have some choice about the ones to use. Any time you give your child some responsibility in the decision-making process, the exercise will be more personal and will have a greater meaning for her.

TELEGRAM

PURPOSE: This game provides practice in summarizing and in note taking.

MATERIALS NEEDED: Schoolbook, magazine, or newspaper, paper, and pencils.

NUMBER OF PLAYERS: 3 or more.

TIME: Allow 15 to 30 minutes.

SKILLS DEVELOPED: This game will give your child a head start on the skills he will need in middle school and high school. He will need to be able to take notes on information he hears in class and reads at home. As parents, we usually don't give too much attention to note taking as a skill; we just expect our children to know how to do it. This game provides guidelines and encourages him to rewrite written information in a type of shorthand that will have meaning for him.

HOW TO PLAY: The object of the game is to rewrite a sentence in as few words as possible, keeping the meaning of the sentence clear. One player locates a sentence in a newspaper, book, or magazine and reads the sentence aloud to the other players. All players then rewrite the same sentence in as few words as possible. For example, *The Japanese government plans to export more cars to the United States* becomes *More Japanese cars coming to U.S.* All players read their sentences aloud and vote on which sentence is the clearest using the fewest words. This game encourages good sportsmanship and fair play.

HINTS AND VARIATIONS: This could be a good way to help your child take homework notes. Use his schoolbook for the game and have some fun while getting the homework done. He might think you are doing some of the work for him, but you are actually showing him, by example, an important study skill.

You could also make the game more like a telegram. Each player would start out with an imaginary amount of money, say $2. Five cents would be subtracted for each word used in the rewritten sentence. The person with the most money left at the end of the each round is the winner.

MATH GAMES

THE STOCK MARKET

PURPOSE: This game encourages your child to practice addition, multiplication, and subtraction skills in an exciting and practical arena.

MATERIALS NEEDED: The New York Stock Exchange report from the financial pages of the Sunday newspaper, paper, pencils, and file folders.

NUMBER OF PLAYERS: Any number can play.

TIME: Allow 30 minutes.

SKILLS DEVELOPED: This game encourages your child to practice math skills in a fun way. She will see that math can relate to many aspects of her life and the ability to manipulate numbers can be very important after she graduates. Everyone needs to balance a checkbook, some of us buy stocks or bonds, and everyone shops for groceries and tries to live within a budget.

She will be risking "play" money based on information she has learned in school or from the news on television or in the newspapers. She will become more alert to world events and how they can affect economy.

HOW TO PLAY: The object of the game is to be the one to make the most "play" money in the stock market over the course of one week. The players choose a target amount of money each player is allowed to "spend." Players examine the Sunday financial page of the newspaper, using the New York Stock Exchange report to choose five different stocks. The stock name abbreviations are listed in the left-hand columns.

If players decide they will spend $10,000 each, each player must then decide how much money she will spend on each of the five stocks. One player might decide to spend $2,000 each for Coca Cola, IBM, AT&T, Gillette, and CBS.

She must then find the prices for each of her stocks in the right-hand column of the exchange report. Round fractions of ½ and more up and those below ½ down. For example, Coca Cola might be listed at 51 ¾ per share; round the cost up to $52. By dividing $2,000 by 52, she will discover she can purchase 38 whole shares. Players must purchase whole shares only.

At $34 per share, she could buy 58 shares of AT&T. IBM would cost her $131 per share, and she could buy 15 shares. At $73 per share, she could buy 27 shares of Gillette. She could buy 11 shares of CBS at $179 per share. Because you cannot buy fractions of shares, the total "spent" will not be exactly $10,000.

After each player has selected her stocks and has decided how many shares of each she will "buy," she places her calculations and selections in a file folder.

The following Sunday, she will find the current price of her stocks and multiply it by her number of shares. She will then add together each of her stock holdings to see if she has more or less money than when she started.

The player who makes the most money wins.

HINTS AND VARIATIONS: If you save the stock pages over two Sundays, the game can be played one evening by checking both day's reports. This game provides a good opportunity to encourage your child to read the business pages of the newspaper and to become involved in what is happening in particular industries in order to decide which stocks she will purchase when playing.

For those who are not familiar with the abbreviations listed in the daily reports, *The Standard and Poor's Stock Guide,* available in local libraries, includes the abbreviations for each company, the price range over a fifteen-year period, and the primary business of each company.

Even though we were not spending real money, my boys enjoyed this game so much that they could not wait a full week to find out how their stocks were doing. They checked their holdings each day.

WEATHER FORECASTING

PURPOSE: This game helps your child see how math is related to the real world.

MATERIALS NEEDED: You will need the weather charts from the newspaper. Save them over a period of a week. You will also need paper and pencils.

NUMBER OF PLAYERS: 2 or more.

TIME: Allow 15 to 20 minutes.

SKILLS DEVELOPED: Math is more than just putting numbers together. It involves looking for patterns in information and making predictions based on that information. By using actual weather charts for these problems your child will be able to test his predictions of real weather trends and patterns, and he will have a better idea of how math can apply to many aspects of his life.

Applying math involves taking risks and making assumptions based on information you already have. This game allows for immediate feedback regarding predictions and helps your child formulate information in preparation for future guesses.

HOW TO PLAY: The object of the game is to choose the city with the highest average temperature over the course of one week. Each player looks at the temperature ranges on Monday's temperature chart and selects a city. Each player much choose a different city. By examining the chart for several days, he can get an idea which cities usually have high temperatures. You can also use this as an opportunity to look at a map of the United States and discuss which cities might be hotter due to their locations.

Once the players have selected their cities, they record the high temperatures for their city each day of the week. At the end of the week, they add the daily temperatures together and then divide by 7 to get an average temperature for the week. Players compare totals, and the player who selected the city with the highest average temperature wins. For example, player 1 chooses *Albuquerque*; player 2 selects *Dallas*; and player 3 chooses *New Orleans*. The daily temperatures for *Albuquerque* are *70, 69, 71, 68, 75, 73, 70*; the average temperature for the week in *Albuquerque* would be *71*. Remainders of 5 and over should be rounded up to the next degree; those with remainders under 5 should be rounded down to the next number. The players for *Dallas* and *New Orleans* perform the same calculations and all players compare results to see which city has the highest average temperature for the week.

HINTS AND VARIATIONS: The information on the weather charts can be used in many ways, so allow your child to come up with different games using the same information. For example, you can each predict which city will have the highest, or lowest, or greatest change in temperature on a particular day. You can use the numbers of the temperature chart to make up problems and have other players solve the problems. Don't limit yourself, and use a calculator if necessary.

This game also gives your child some understanding of geographical differences.

ABOUT THE
AUTHORS

CHERYL GERSON TUTTLE, M.ED., has been both a parent and teacher for more than twenty years. She holds a master's degree in reading and language arts and a bachelor's degree in education and is a Special Education Coordinator for the Marblehead (Massachusetts) Public Schools. She is the mother of two sons and has a grandchild on the way. She is coauthor of *Parenting a Child with a Learning Disability*; *Challenging Voices: Writings by, for, and About People with Learning Disabilities*; and *Parenting a Child with a Behavior Problem*.

PENNY HUTCHINS PAQUETTE is an educational writer and a librarian for the Marblehead (Massachusetts) Public Schools. She has three children and two grandchildren. She is the coauthor of *Parenting a Child with a Learning Disability* and *Parenting a Child with a Behavior Problem*.